LEADING ASSESSMENT FOR STUDENT SUCCESS

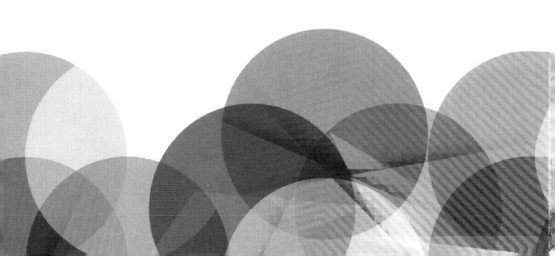

LEADING ASSESSMENT FOR STUDENT SUCCESS

Ten Tenets That Change Culture and Practice in Student Affairs

Edited by Rosie Phillips Bingham,

Daniel A. Bureau, and Amber Garrison Duncan

Foreword by Marilee J. Bresciani Ludvik

STERLING, VIRGINIA

Published by Stylus Publishing, LLC.
22883 Quicksilver Drive
Sterling, Virginia 20166-2102

Library of Congress Cataloging-in-Publication Data
Leading assessment for student success : ten tenets that change
culture and practice in student affairs / edited by Rosie Phillips
Bingham, Daniel Bureau, and Amber Garrison Duncan ; foreword
by Marilee Bresciani. -- First edition.
    pages cm
  Includes index.
  ISBN 978-1-62036-222-8 (pbk. : acid free paper)
  ISBN 978-1-62036-221-1 (cloth : acid free paper)
  ISBN 978-1-62036-223-5 (library networkable e-edition)
  ISBN 978-1-62036-224-2 (consumer e-edition)
    1. Student affairs services--United States--Evaluation.   2.
Education, Higher--United States--Evaluation.   I. Bingham,
Rosie.   II. Bureau, Daniel, 1976-   III. Duncan, Amber Garrison,
1976-
  LB2342.92.L45 2016
  371.4--dc23
                                                2015020330
13-digit ISBN: 978-1-62036-221-1 (cloth)
13-digit ISBN: 978-1-62036-222-8 (paperback)
13-digit ISBN: 978-1-62036-223-5 (library networkable e-edition)
13-digit ISBN: 978-1-62036-224-2 (consumer e-edition)

Printed in the United States of America

All first editions printed on acid-free paper
that meets the American National Standards Institute
Z39-48 Standard.

Bulk Purchases

Quantity discounts are available for use in workshops and for
staff development.
Call 1-800-232-0223

First Edition, 2015

10   9   8   7   6   5   4   3   2   1

CONTENTS

FOREWORD

As I complete the reading of the most recent draft of this book, I recall a conversation I had with Eric Rivera, San Diego State University's vice president for student affairs. We had reviewed a myriad of findings generated from outcomes-based assessment, competency-based assessment, and institutional research processes and were discussing the importance of continuing to elevate the holistic student learning and development conversation in light of the challenge of connecting outcomes-based assessment findings, outcomes-based program review findings, or competency-based assessment findings to performance indicators and other accountability measures. This conversation affirmed that the very real challenge of connecting meaningful outcomes-based or competency-based data to performance indicators would continue, particularly with current and anticipated accountability legislation. In light of that conversation, this book brings to our attention the urgency for student affairs professionals to engage fully in holistic assessment practices.

Many student affairs professionals provide direct opportunities for students to learn and develop, as well as opportunities for students to apply their learning and development. Telling the story of how well we facilitate holistic learning and development and how learning and development can be assessed and evaluated should foster awareness of the importance of collaborative design, delivery, and responsible evaluation as we conduct student affairs programs. Telling this story using data can illustrate the key role that a student affairs professional plays in advancing intentional student learning and development. However, telling this story requires that leadership invest in all of the dimensions of creating an environment focused on dynamic, integrated learning; development; and reflective practice.

I have often joked, "Assessment can't fix leadership." All the great data—regardless of how sound the processes were that collected those data—can't move leadership to use that information if they don't want to do so. What makes this book so compelling is that each chapter is written in collaboration with a senior student affairs officer. Readers benefit from viewing perspectives shared by senior student affairs officers *and* student affairs assessment scholars. Through sharing good practices, senior leadership can gain practical examples and advice on how to infuse assessment into the infrastructure of student affairs. Surely this book will prove beneficial to those who peruse its pages; it provides both practical advice and intriguing concepts to consider.

This book explains how to tell the story of assessment while engaging each student affairs team member on your campus, whether he or she is the senior student affairs officer or a frontline professional. Each chapter builds on the previous one, making the case for why assessment matters and explaining how to implement assessment practice so that inquiry becomes a priority, deeply embedded into the daily work of all who believe in and contribute to student success.

This book shares various ways to evaluate implementation of student success theory and practice in a manner that leads to improving relevant outcomes. Upon reading it, you will likely gain ideas to cultivate a culture of inquiry along with important means to communicate results to stakeholders and garner their feedback for prioritizing recommendations. This book provides a "how to" in making assessment an integral practice of the student affairs profession.

Outcomes-based and competency-based assessment is needed, now more than ever, in order to make sense of the accountability measures for which leaders are held responsible. A primary component of sound evidence-based decision making requires all team members to engage in quality reflection and dialogue with multiple constituents. In the case of higher education, that includes students. We know that students must play a primary role in their own learning and development journey and therefore they must play a primary role in the assessment process. However, the inclusion of students in this dynamic process won't happen unless leaders foster student engagement. Leadership is necessary if any transformation is to arise from any learning and development data.

What we understand from transformational leadership research is that (a) everyone leads whether he or she is aware of it or not (Larry Ward, personal communication, September 26, 2014) and (b) a drop in productivity occurs whenever organizations engage in significant lines of inquiry or significant change processes (Laurie Cameron, personal communication, October 23, 2014). Leaders of an organization (which, according to Larry Ward, would be all of you) cannot produce at the level (read: quantity) that they once did when they are investigating a new line of inquiry or implementing data-informed changes.

When student affairs professionals integrate assessment practice, meaningful reflection on the data gathered, and collaborative discussions about what the data mean and what changes they could inform, these processes simply take time. Creating collaborations that can lead to designing improvements in holistic student learning and development requires time. People may need professional development release time to best understand how to connect outcomes-based and competency-based data to performance indicators, to say nothing of time dedicated to learning how to engage in effective assessment practices.

Quantity of productivity may decline as reflective assessment practices are systematically put into place. Leadership must hold the space for a potential decline in productivity so that quality assessment, meaningful reflection, and collaborative meaning making of the data collected can occur. It is my hope that the leaders (again, all of you) who are reading this book are the leaders who have that kind of courage—the courage to hold space for transformation to occur. If so, I invite you to read this book and fully engage in the lessons our colleagues share. Explore how the ideas presented in these pages may be adapted and taken up within your organization. Then, collaboratively execute and enjoy the fruits of your investment in meaningful inquiry.

Marilee J. Bresciani Ludvik, PhD
Professor, postsecondary education, San Diego State University
April 29, 2015

ACKNOWLEDGMENTS

We'd like to acknowledge all of the dedicated professionals who have worked tirelessly in student affairs assessment for your foresight and vision in prioritizing this work as a part of our profession. We extend a special thank you to chapter contributors; we couldn't have produced this book without you. We especially dedicate this book to our families: John and Akil (Rosie), Amanda and Elise (Dan), and John (Amber).

Rosie Phillips Bingham,
Daniel A. Bureau, and
Amber Garrison Duncan

INTRODUCTION

Daniel A. Bureau and Rosie Phillips Bingham

takeholders in higher education, both internally and externally, have increasingly called on the profession of student affairs to focus attention on and implement an evidence-based culture. For decades, these stakeholders have issued urgent appeals for including assessment in a more formal way in divisions of student affairs. Across higher education, administrators want to be certain that every dollar spent has a high return on investment in order to benefit students. Stakeholders want to be assured that the programs and services involved in student affairs are highly effective and efficient in contributing to the mission of higher education. Not only parents and families, but also donors and federal and state agencies are demanding accountability for their dollars. However, the demand is not just from others; it is part of who we are as a profession. Most student affairs professionals we know want to provide highly effective and excellent programs and services that help students succeed in college as well as beyond graduation. As professionals, we need to tell our stories in ways that use evidence to reflect our influence on student retention, graduation, and overall success. These goals are why we wrote this book, to provide a direct and practical message about creating a culture of assessment in student affairs.

What has been missing are directions for division leaders about *how* to create and sustain such a culture. The authors in this volume are all experienced senior-level leaders who have established programs that have led to a culture of evidence-based practice. Grounded in assessment literature, the authors have outlined ten tenets designed to focus senior leaders on committing to student learning and assessment, to leading culture change, and to implementing sound assessment practices.

The tenets are outlined here for ease of reference and so the reader may begin to understand the structure of this book. The chapters are further grouped around three overall themes: "Philosophical Commitments" (Chapters 1–2), "Division Leadership and Culture" (Chapters 3–6), and "Sound Assessment Practices" (Chapters 7–10). We end with an epilogue that serves as a summary and a nod to the future. A major premise of the book is that the senior student affairs officer (SSAO) must be the primary leader and spokesperson for this effort. The SSAO sets the tone and provides leadership to the team participating in implementing a comprehensive assessment program. Therefore, each chapter/tenet listed begins with a testimony or thoughts from an SSAO about the tenet addressed in the chapter.

Chapter 1:   Tenet One: Understand the "Why" of Assessment
Chapter 2:   Tenet Two: Commit to Student Learning as a Primary Focus
Chapter 3:   Tenet Three: Lay the Foundation for a Sustainable Assessment Culture
Chapter 4:   Tenet Four: Develop Strategies to Engage Staff in a Commitment to Assessment
Chapter 5:   Tenet Five: Implement Accountability and Support Structures to Encourage Assessment
Chapter 6:   Tenet Six: Anchor Cultural Change
Chapter 7:   Tenet Seven: Develop Assessment Plans
Chapter 8:   Tenet Eight: Connect Assessment Plans to Institutional and Divisional Goals
Chapter 9:   Tenet Nine: Determine the Appropriate Methods for Assessing Programs and Services
Chapter 10: Tenet Ten: Disseminate Data to Leverage buy-in and Promote Utility to the Campus Community

In Chapter 1 Bingham and Bureau set the stage for *why* assessment matters. They clarify terms so that readers understand the differences among concepts such as assessment, evaluation, and research. Although research is a component of any useful assessment program, this book is solidly focused on assessment and using evidence to evaluate and inform decision-making. The authors provide a brief historical and professional overview that demonstrates the role of an evidence-based culture in even the early formation and professionalization of student affairs.

If assessment is essential, then learning is core. Chapter 2 opens with SSAO Henley clearly declaring that student affairs professionals are educators. He states, "After all, we are members of the academy, a learning organization, and we work in a learning environment" (p. 23). The business of the academy is learning. Chapter author Barber states, "We must implement effective assessment practices to document how our work is actively promoting college student learning" (p. 24). He calls on student affairs professionals to adopt a learning paradigm and to understand the role of theories in shaping and assessing student learning. He goes on to provide summaries of two theories that readers will find clear and helpful. Furthermore, this chapter provides resources that can be used to formulate and assess student learning and outcomes.

The third tenet, in Chapter 3, explains the need to educate staff in divisions of student affairs about the culture of assessment. Garrison Duncan and Holmes talk about the importance of the leader influencing staff to become part of the assessment movement. They say that it is important to be cognizant of the fact that many in student affairs have not been educated in assessment methods and are therefore embarking on learning a new skill or process, which can be daunting. They provide introductory remarks about the four elements necessary to start a culture of assessment: commitment, consistency, connection, and communication.

Woods and Schafer maintain that it is essential to get staff "buy-in" in order to implement an assessment culture, which is the focus of Chapter 4. The SSAO must understand the unique culture at his or her institution in order to understand what it will take to get the entire staff on board and committed. They maintain that the SSAO must create an environment of trust, accountability, and transparency. Equally important is building strong interpersonal and collaborative relationships among the staff.

Chapter 5 focuses on the broad tactics of how the SSAO strengthens culture. Burris Hester and Kepler use Sanford's classic student development theory of challenge and support to focus on specific approaches to ensuring that assessment is a part of a division's culture. As assessment becomes less of a nice thing to do and more of a necessity, implementing approaches to rewarding staff while also holding underperformers accountable will be vital.

In Chapter 6, the final chapter in "Part Two: Division Leadership and Culture," Adams-Gaston and Kennedy-Phillips elucidate the importance of sustaining a culture of evidence. Building on the same elements discussed in Chapter 3 on starting a culture, they emphasize the need for commitment, consistency, connection, and communication to sustain it. Efforts to develop, implement, and sustain an assessment culture must be consistent. We must remain committed to assessment and communicate to internal and external stakeholders in a way that connects with their needs and tells the student affairs story.

The next part of the book, "Sound Assessment Practices," summarizes the essential assessment practices that senior leaders should be aware of in order to effectively reinforce them along with the culture strategies previously discussed. Although there are many books on assessment practices, the authors of this section have sought to provide SSAOs with practices that ensure assessments of services, programs, and student learning are organized and systematized. In Chapter 7, Roberts makes the case for establishing an assessment cycle that is linear, predictable, consistent, and stable. She maintains that the assessment cycle must be tied to the information needed by internal and external constituencies, including the timing of programs, services, and budget cycles. In this practical chapter, readers will find examples of assessment cycle templates that can be applied across departments in student affairs.

Chapter 8 calls for linking student affairs assessment plans with the institution's mission and strategic plan. Blaisdell and Chamberlain state that it is the strategic plan that ensures "that people, facilities, capital, and other resources are deployed most effectively" (p. 96) to maximally affect student success. They explain that culture is an important consideration when connecting assessment to divisional and institutional strategic plans. These authors help the reader understand the language of strategic planning and the importance of tying the student affairs strategic plan to the overall college or university strategic plan. Linking assessment plans in this way should provide information that helps the division to know if work is fulfilling the vision, mission, and strategic plan of the overall institution as well as the division.

Equally important are the tools used to gather the data as outlined in the assessment plans. We must utilize diverse approaches to collecting evidence within student affairs programs, which requires that staff understand how approaches to collecting evidence differ based on the questions we have to answer. Additionally, SSAOs must be prepared to ask for qualitative and quantitative as well as direct and indirect methods of assessment. In Chapter 9, Wise offers building blocks to help determine types of assessments that will be effective in producing data about programs, services, participants, and learning. She calls attention to methods that allow us to go beyond the typical survey and suggests using such approaches as observation, rubrics, tests or quizzes, document analysis, and so on. She champions mixed methods that rely on quantitative and qualitative approaches to measurements. She underscores how much of what student affairs staff already do in their day-to-day work could be considered aspects of assessment practice.

Data on a shelf are useless. That is the position of Christakis and Demeter in Chapter 10, which concerns itself with how to publish and make data resonate with key decision makers. Data give voice to the experiences of students that can be shared with stakeholders in ways that demonstrate the impact of student affairs. The authors offer the following essential elements for effective information-sharing: ensuring information authenticity, knowing your audience, presenting user-friendly information, using high-quality visuals, choosing outlets wisely, not becoming stale, making information actionable, and following up. Christakis and Demeter argue it is the SSAO who is the most compelling champion and communicator of student affairs assessment information. The chapter ends with examples of very compelling best practices for sharing data.

Lastly, Garrison Duncan and Kruger, speaking specifically of larger higher education priorities and initiatives that will drive the work of student affairs, provide thoughts on the future of assessment in the book's epilogue. Affirming the previous ten tenets, they look to how the evolution of student affairs assessment, discussed in Chapter 1, will continue to become a part of the culture of this field. Through her work with the Lumina Foundation, Garrison Duncan has seen how higher education has been sometimes responsive but at other times inactive toward societal priorities. She advocates for student affairs to continue to take on the tough topics, collect evidence on student learning in the cocurriculum, and demonstrate where our services have made a difference for student success.

PART ONE

PHILOSOPHICAL COMMITMENTS

"Until one is committed, there is hesitancy, the chance to draw back, always ineffectiveness. Concerning all acts of initiative and creation, there is one elementary truth the ignorance of which kills countless ideas and splendid plans: that the moment one definitely commits oneself, then providence moves too."

W. H. Murray, *The Scottish Himalayan Expedition*, 1951

"Unless commitment is made, there are only promises and hopes—but no plans."

Peter F. Drucker, *The Five Most Important Questions Self-Assessment Tool*, 2010

What it means to commit to assessment and student learning has evolved in the twenty-first century for all of higher education. As a reminder and as a call to action, the chapters that follow in this section provide background about why assessment is so important today and the necessity for an easy-to-access theoretical framework for student learning. Over and over we hear that senior leaders must demonstrate an unwavering commitment to these two philosophical concepts that can then create the space for culture and practice changes. With these two commitments, senior leaders can center all work on the student and provide a holistic learning experience that leads to greater student success.

1

TENET ONE: UNDERSTAND THE "WHY" OF ASSESSMENT

Rosie Phillips Bingham and Daniel A. Bureau

SSAO's Perspective

Rosie Phillips Bingham

Student affairs professionals have always been dedicated and committed to the development of students through programs, services, and interpersonal connections with students. As professionals, we believe we are critical to helping students achieve their goals. We believe that we help students learn skills that are essential for their success in their professional and personal lives.

This has been the student affairs rhetoric. I believe this to be true. But how do I know?

Assessment is critical to measuring the effect student affairs has on student success. How do I prove this to stakeholders: colleagues across the campus, the students we serve, parents, and external constituents ranging from donors to the federal government? How do I know what impact those programs—from short onetime experiences to ongoing learning opportunities—have on student learning, retention, and overall success? How do I know that having a division of student affairs matters in the larger higher education arena?

These questions led me to begin to work on changing the culture in the division of student affairs when I became the senior student affairs officer (SSAO) in 2003. I wanted us to take our culture of providing excellent programs and services and integrate a culture of curiosity. I wanted us to infuse assessment into our work in a way that would give us evidence that our programs contribute to institutional and divisional goals. We need great programs and services that really make a difference. So I decided to use all the research and scholarship that called on student affairs professionals to focus our efforts on learning and student involvement as the vehicle to help students succeed and graduate. I decided to focus on assessment of what we do.

Assessment is a key to understanding that both learning and purposeful involvement are occurring. As a result of assessing our programs, evidence emerges that tells our story in a way that has meaning and impact. Our story can be explained quantitatively in terms of magnitude, not just anecdotally. Our story can be told in a sophisticated, empirical manner or it can be told in a way that makes sense to all. Regardless of the approach we take to telling the story, an essential part of the student affairs storyline is evidence to ensure we make a difference. I embarked on what has been a 10-year effort to infuse assessment into the work of all in our division.

At the University of Memphis we developed the motto "Students learning through engagement and involvement." We also created a position entitled director of student learning and assessment. Early on, we provided training to staff and took small steps as we began to make assessment a part of the very fabric of life and work in student affairs. We began to see real results in some departments. Some of those results netted bigger financial investments from the university into the work we were doing in the division. Ten years later, I believe that we must continue to answer the "How do I know?" questions. I believe that the case for assessment is increasing throughout the academy. I believe that student affairs divisions that fail to collect meaningful evidence of contributions may be facing extinction. I believe in the why of assessment, and that's the focus of this chapter.

Always the Struggle: How to Tell the Story

Throughout our history, the field of student affairs has struggled with telling its story in a way that speaks to decision makers; however, this task has always been a part of our work. Reviewing early guiding documents such as *The Student Personnel Point of View* (1937) indicates that student affairs professionals have long been tasked with "carrying on studies designed to evaluate and improve . . . functions and services" (American Council on Education, 1994, p. 42). In fact, an analysis of guiding documents conducted by Evans and Reason (2001) revealed that an orientation toward empirically grounded initiatives in student affairs work was found in 11 of 13 guiding documents from 1937 to 1999. Some think the empirical approach to work in student affairs is new, but it has long been part of the DNA of our work.

Additionally, the development of the Council for the Advancement of Standards in Higher Education (CAS) in 1979 came from a need to unite student affairs practitioners in a shared pursuit of excellence. By nature, the CAS standards were driven by interassociation collaboration across diverse student affairs functions. Such collaboration was founded on the development of shared and distinctive standards for functional areas within student affairs and higher education. The ability to document how these standards were actualized becomes tantamount to their implementation. As a result, since their inception, the CAS standards have been widely applied for assessment within student affairs (Arminio, 2009).

Many point to Upcraft and Schuh's 1996 work, *Assessment in Student Affairs: A Guide for Practitioners*, as the turning point for prioritizing assessment within modern-day student affairs. In fact, the foreword to that text may sound very familiar to you as you read this chapter. Upcraft and Schuh (1996) explained:

> For many reasons . . . student affairs needs high quality and comprehensive assessment programs. Unfortunately, among staff in student affairs, assessment is an unknown quantity at best, or at the worst, it is misunderstood and misused. It has been our experience that while everyone in student affairs would agree that assessment is important, too often it is considered a low priority and never conducted in any systematic, comprehensive way. (p. 4)

Almost 20 years later, how far has the needle moved? In some contexts, assessment is a part of the culture of student affairs practice. In others it might be an afterthought or something that is done without much planning or intention. Assessment is inherently intentional and focused on predetermined outcomes for students. Stories upon stories can be told about how our field has not been able to prioritize and integrate assessment in its day-to-day work. Such a reality means that even good intentions have not resulted in assessment being well integrated into the purpose of student affairs for the last 100 years.

Today's field demands more of professionals and many are not meeting the expectations of modern-day student affairs (Kuk, Cobb, & Forrest, 2007). Assessment has moved beyond a trend and has become a framework for practice rather than an add-on activity (Schuh & Gansemer-Topf, 2010). The field continues to move to a place where assessment is a professional priority and a necessary competency (American College Personnel Association & National Association of Student Personnel Administrators, 2010). There are numerous books, monographs, chapters, and articles written about student affairs assessment. Any review of convention workshop offerings from any functional area of student affairs likely boasts numerous offerings in assessment. Professional associations have affinity groups that come together for the sake of learning about assessment (the American College Personnel Association has a commission; the National Association of Student Personnel Administrators has its Knowledge Community). Finally, a new but emerging association focused primarily on the needs of professionals who conduct student affairs assessment work was established in 2008. Student Affairs Assessment Leaders (SAAL) now has over 400 members. Assessment is our history, our current reality, and essential to our future.

Why Assessment Matters

Some individuals inside and outside of higher education have questioned the importance and criticality of student affairs in the process of students learning course content and obtaining degrees. Answering the question "How critical is student affairs to the higher education enterprise?" has never been more important, and using assessment practices to address that question has become an essential part of modern-day student affairs work (Bresciani, 2010). Assessment practices that have become vital are those that document program and service participation, explain students' perceptions of the quality of services and programs, and demonstrate the impact of the student affairs function on student learning, retention, and graduation. This chapter explains why assessment matters to student affairs work as well as the differentiation among assessment, research, and evaluation, making the case that assessment matters because it has long been a part of our field's work and will continue to become more and more important to the future success of student affairs on college and university campuses.

Responding well to questions about the criticality of student affairs to the higher education enterprise is important for two reasons: it provides evidence of both the efficiencies and the effectiveness of our programs but also makes these qualities transparent to stakeholders, most notably the American public. Efficiency in higher education has never been more important, and its influence on student affairs is significant. Most student affairs divisions function with limited resources; therefore, the professionals who manage those programs want to be certain that programs and services are efficiently and effectively helping students to develop and succeed.

Funding formulas have changed in many states. Historically, funding for public colleges and universities for the education of students was based on the number of students enrolled in the institution. More recently a number of states began to allocate funding based on the number of students who are retained and graduate—an outcomes funding approach. In an outcomes- and performance-based environment, every student program and service is evaluated for its contribution to the bottom line of increasing student retention and graduation. It has become important for student affairs professionals to expand the number of programs and services that lead to retention and graduation. In such situations, demonstrating the return on investment for student affairs becomes especially important. It is the assessment process that will allow student affairs professionals to identify the educational experiences that do enrich students' lives and improve retention and graduation.

Effective assessment programs will allow student affairs professionals to analyze, discuss, and use data to make informed decisions about appropriate programs and services that lead to student success. So what might this look like in practice as a division enacts its assessment program? Consider some functional area examples: Student activities wants to know how to attract future students to programs, whether current students are satisfied with the programs, and what impact programs have had on past students. Campus recreation wants to demonstrate the impact of participation on student retention or how fitness training correlates with academic success, as well as what students learn when refereeing intramural sports teams or the best value in fitness equipment the department purchases. Career services questions how to engage students early with staff in order to be maximally effective in helping students find jobs or how to help document the student learning that occurs through internships and work experiences on and off campus. In each area of student affairs, professionals should know the impact of their work on student learning, retention, and graduation.

Efficiency is about how our programs, resources, and services reflect institutional goals in a manner that appropriately uses resources. One goal of any college or university is student learning and development. It has been over a decade since *Learning Reconsidered* (Keeling & Associates, 2004) provided the direction for a renewed dialogue on ensuring student affairs programs, resources, and services contribute to student learning and success. As the field has risen to the call for an emphasis on student learning (Barber & Bureau, 2012; Reason & Broido, 2010), professionals must define—within the context of their practice—what it is that students must learn and provide evidence that their involvement in said activities matters (Collins & Roberts, 2012). As this focus has moved to the forefront of student affairs work, assessment of the ability to educate students is arguably our field's most important assessment priority; our rhetoric must be matched with evidence. Torres and Walbert (2010) asserted, "The use of high-quality data to support decisions about policies, programs, and practices is increasingly expected. This climate of evidence-based accountability promises to be particularly challenging for student affairs" (p. 10). The future is now. We must meet the challenge and our field needs to increasingly attend to the demands of our public and provide evidence that we are doing so.

Providing evidence of our value to stakeholders is another reason why assessment in student affairs matters. Internal constituents, such as university administrators, want to be certain that the programs and services in student affairs support the mission, goals, and values of the university (Bresciani, 2010). Another area in which evidence is important to our stakeholders is documenting the outcomes of participation in activities that our field believes contribute to a student's ability to be a good citizen and trusted worker in our global society (Schuh & Gansemer-Topf, 2010). Student success in college matters to our society; such an outcome is important to employers, boards of regents/trustees, potential students, parents, donors, and other external audiences. For example, employers are interested in students who are able to write, think critically, manage various types of interpersonal relationships, solve problems, and work independently and interdependently (Hart Research Associates, 2013). Student affairs programs can significantly impact each of these learning outcomes. However, in order to ensure such outcomes are met, assessment programs are essential. Employers want to know which educational and student affairs programs can deliver them a workforce with the requisite skills for the positions and environments into which they are hired (Schuh & Gansemer-Topf, 2010). Assessment results can provide them with the data.

It is also important that student affairs professionals be seen as vital collaborators in students' holistic development and learning (Collins & Roberts, 2012). Student success requires a team effort on the part of staff and faculty: the tired old paradigm of us versus them serves our students poorly and student affairs professionals should quickly get over this barrier. Student affairs matters, but we have to recognize how we contribute to student learning in partnership with our faculty colleagues. Unless we are connecting our student programs, resources, and services directly to student outcomes as defined at the level of credit-bearing courses, by major programs, or in the college/university itself, then we should accept that faculty who teach and conduct research are why students are coming to college.

However, there are so many ways student affairs professionals can be good partners in the journey. Although faculty members often do not understand what professionals in student affairs do, they certainly understand the concept of student learning. When professors see the demonstration that student affairs programs and services support their efforts inside the classroom they can begin to understand that everyone is on the team and a part of the process. In fact, if the assessment plan is robust enough, faculty members may even be able to offer suggestions to improve student affairs programs. For example, given that critical thinking is an essential outcome of the bachelor's degree, by focusing on how both the curriculum and cocurriculum contribute to this outcome, faculty and staff can better partner to create seamless learning environments for students. The faculty member might see that a program offered through student affairs effectively moves students toward improvements in critical thinking. The faculty member may be able to use the program as a part of his or her course and further suggest to the program provider how to extend the program to create a powerful synergy between classroom instruction and student affairs programs. Assessment results should inform the student, faculty member, and student affairs professional about what the student is learning and how that learning is contributing to the student's success. This is modern-day student affairs work. This is collaboration based on evidence in which all parties know what they need to do in order to make the difference needed.

The larger public wants to know about such an impact as well. Assessment is even more critical for student affairs at a time when external forces are questioning the effectiveness of higher education in general. During the last decade, most people working in higher education have become familiar with the terms *affordability* and *accountability*. Federal and state policy makers, as well as the public, have been asking colleges and universities to provide evidence that they are educating all citizens for the workforce at an affordable price. One of the most important nationwide trends has been the call from President Barack Obama to make higher education more affordable with fewer "frills." In his 2013 State of the Union speech, President Obama called "Congress to consider value, affordability, and student outcomes in making determinations about which colleges and universities receive access to federal student aid" (Council for Higher Education Accreditation, 2013). A recent Gallup poll (Lumina Foundation, 2013) reported that 67% of respondents said higher education institutions should reduce tuition and fees. Further, Governor Rick Perry of Texas asserted that colleges should be funded at a much lower rate, and funding should be based on job placement. The governor even went as far as to issue a challenge for state universities to offer a degree that costs no more than $10,000 (Scholarships.com, 2014). A survey administered at Northeastern University revealed most Americans believe a college education is more important now than it was in previous generations. However, 73% agreed they would like no-frills programs that did "not include extras such as ability to live in dorms and the use of college facilities like the gym" (Northeastern University, 2013). It is evident that higher education must document its value and convince elected officials and the public that the time and money invested matter. In student affairs we must demonstrate internally and externally that we have a significant impact on student learning, retention, graduation, and even the acquisition of jobs after graduation. Assessment can help us do that.

Yet, some student affairs professionals still tremble at the mention of assessment. Some respond this way due to perceptions of what assessment is, how assessment is done, and out of fear of negative consequences. The next part of this chapter focuses on clarifying terminology and explaining the reasons behind assessment as everyday practice in student affairs.

Clarifying Our Language and Approaches to Assessment

Assessment can be defined as a process for gathering and analyzing data in order to make an informed decision about how a program/activity/function is performing (Upcraft & Schuh, 1996). It is important to differentiate between assessment and the processes of research and evaluation, as the distinction is often what paralyzes professionals who have good intentions to assess their programs but believe their competence is insufficient. The distinction can be as simple as the intent.

Information gathered from assessment is properly used for internal improvement and development of quality programs, resources, and services. As we have already stated, if we can provide evidence that programs matter to the learning and experiences of students, we can then make the case that student affairs has a valuable contribution to make to the academy. The overall purpose of assessment is to examine a single context or specific program to determine if it achieves its goals; it is not intended to prove theories. The intent is to use data internally to inform decisions, understanding that the limitations include a lack of generalizability outside of one context, and that decisions are made best when using more than one form of evidence.

Research contributes by creating a body of literature and building on theoretical knowledge that supports the contributions of student affairs. Upcraft and Schuh (1996) define *research* as a process that "guides theory development and tests concepts" (p. 19). Although research methods of data collection and analysis can be similar to those used during assessment, student affairs professionals who conduct assessment are tasked with collecting and analyzing information to make decisions, not necessarily to prove a theory or concept. The intention of research may be to create statements of generalizability outside of the specific context of an institution. Additionally, the amount of evidence needed for valid and reliable research generally exceeds what is required for assessment, so, for example, a smaller N or lower response rate on a survey may be acceptable.

Unfortunately, the distinction between assessment and research is one of the biggest factors in professionals' discomfort when they hear *assessment*. Following best practices without questioning their effectiveness is far more comfortable. When the term *assessment* is heard, many people think of research and immediately consider it impossible for them to be engaged in the assessment process. However, professionals must think critically about the implications of their work. They must use assessment results to shape the direction of the next set of services and programs.

The distinction between assessment and research begs further explanation, especially because most people leading divisions of student affairs were trained in research by way of the doctorate. For example, an assessment of a disability resources program might ask, "Did students who participated in one of the services provided by the department have better term-to-term retention and why?" The information sources may be many—number of students, focus groups, surveys, and so on. Research might ask a different question that compares one theoretical approach to services with another to determine if there is a significant difference between the two: *proving* that one approach to serving students with disabilities has a different (or better) influence than another. Again, assessment can have research-like methodologies but typically does not require the same level of scientific rigor, as it is measuring the direct impact of the program on students in one context instead of creating a generalizable theory for how to approach disability services.

Evaluation comes after the completion of assessment activities and can be defined as "efforts to use assessment to improve institutional, departmental, division, or agency effectiveness" (Upcraft & Schuh, 1996, p. 19). Evaluation of the results allows us to determine if the results of the program were actually of value to the student. For instance, students participating in a program may report a high level of satisfaction; however, the program may not achieve the desired results for student learning. Therefore, the value of the program may not have been achieved. Evaluation could also ask a program to compare its assessment or results against standards. For example, CAS provides standards and guidelines for disability resources. To continue with our example, such a department might look at results it has gleaned over the course of time and evaluate those results against the CAS standards. Evaluation of the resources within the program will help to review a range of department criteria such as effectiveness, managing and reducing costs, and student learning with those resources.

Data for assessment can be collected in numerous ways including observations, surveys, examinations, focus groups, and more formal research processes. Methods should relate to purpose. Therefore, in learner-centered assessment, the focus is on determining what a student has learned and the effectiveness of the services and programs designed for the learner. For example, a disability resources office may have a program focused on career preparation that includes an assessment of what students learned as a result of a workshop. Assessment of whether students felt the program benefited them versus an examination of which factors contributed to retention and persistence as a result of the program will often require different assessment approaches. Wise explores the range of potential assessment methods in Chapter 9.

An effective assessment program aids the student affairs professional in making decisions about learning outcomes, programs, goals, and processes. Huba and Freed (2000) maintained that there are four fundamental components of assessment: establishing the intended learning outcome, determining and selecting assessment measures, developing the learning experiences that will lead to learning outcomes, and using assessment data to refine the process and improve learning. Student affairs professionals who follow such an assessment process will ensure they are significantly impacting student success and thus positively contributing to retention and graduation. Assessment in student affairs is essential because it helps the professional determine the plan of action for student success.

Assessment should demonstrate that the division of student affairs is aligned with and contributing to achieving the institution's mission and strategic plan. It is critical that SSAOs review their divisional plans, programs, and services to ensure that their assessment plans gather the data to provide evidence of support for the university's mission, values, and strategic plan (Schuh & Gansemer-Topf, 2010). As SSAOs create the case for why assessment matters, they need to develop strategies to ensure that assessment is embedded into the culture of the division.

Once we have a working definition of *assessment*, as well as a better understanding of its diverse purposes and methods, we must ask how we can make assessment a prominent value and practice in the field of student affairs. We might start with the field's traditions and values: Assessment matters because student affairs professionals are concerned with and always have attended to student success (Evans & Reason, 2001). Ironically, although student affairs professionals may fear the emergence of formal assessment, the use of evidence to improve programs has always been a part of our profession.

Conclusion

History tells the story we have inherited; forecasting tells us what could happen. Planning for the future of assessment means that we begin to own our story and determine the future of the field. Assessment matters in student affairs because our internal and external constituents believe we should document our contributions and continually examine ways to improve the quality of our programs, resources, and services (and because we want to know that what we are doing has purpose and is effective). But what does it look like today and in the future to effectively infuse assessment into student affairs work? The remaining chapters in this book explain more about the characteristics of a good student affairs assessment program.

Of course, all of this is based on identifying and enacting priorities: What matters most to student affairs practice in the modern-day environment is how we can know we are doing it well. Modern-day practice reflects a long-time evolution of assessment programs, reflecting the field's increasing focus on learning and its impact on retention and graduation. It has become evident that student affairs is about student learning and professionals serving in the field should identify as educators.

Is this an evolution of our field or an affirmation of our history? Barber and Bureau (2012) explain,

> Although not always positioned as primary, promoting student learning has long been a part of student affairs work. . . . The learning paradigm of student affairs has not necessarily replaced previous professional priorities . . . instead student learning has become the reason for rather than the byproduct of student services and student development. (p. 39)

As student learning has become *the* reason for student affairs work, assessment has become a required approach we use to provide evidence of our contributions to higher education (Collins & Roberts, 2012).

Ultimately, there is a decision to be made. Will student affairs professionals provide evidence that their programs, resources, and services support student learning and development? Will we use such evidence to deliver best practices and to innovate on those best practices so that more students succeed? Will we transform programs so that the next millennium sees even more students graduate as a result of student affairs being able to demonstrate effectiveness in accomplishing institutional missions? Strong leadership at the SSAO level is vital to making this happen. The premise of assessment as a priority for the SSAO is ultimately what drove the authoring of this book.

This chapter explains the function of assessment in student affairs and how assessment, specifically the focus on assessing student learning, has become a vital part of modern-day student affairs work. Through these last pages we have explained the "why" of assessment in student affairs. Next, Barber explores more deeply the importance of student learning within student affairs assessment work.

References

American College Personnel Association & National Association of Student Personnel Administrators. (2010). *ACPA/NASPA professional competency areas for student affairs practitioners.* Washington, DC: Author.

American Council on Education. (1994). *The student personnel point of view, 1937.* Retrieved from https://www.uwsuper.edu/campuslife/news/upload/9-27-11-SPPV.pdf

Arminio, J. (2009). Applying professional standards. In G. S. McClellan, J. Stringer, & Associates (Eds.), *The handbook of student affairs administration* (3rd ed., pp. 187–205). San Francisco, CA: Jossey-Bass.

Barber, J. P., & Bureau, D. A. (2012). Coming into focus: Positioning student learning from *The Student Personnel Point of View* to today. In K. M. Boyle, J. W. Lowery, & J. A. Mueller (Eds.), *Reflections on the 75th anniversary of* The Student Personnel Point of View (pp. 35–40). Washington, DC: American College Personnel Association & College Student Educators International.

Bresciani, M. (2010). Assessment and evaluation. In J. H. Schuh, S. R. Jones, S. R. Harper, & Associates (Eds.), *Student services: A handbook for the profession* (5th ed. pp. 321–334). San Francisco, CA: Jossey-Bass.

Collins, K. M., & Roberts, D. M. (Eds.). (2012). *Learning is not a sprint: Assessing and documenting student leader learning in cocurricular involvement.* Washington, DC: National Association of Student Personnel Administrators.

Council for Higher Education Accreditation. (2013, February 14). *The president's State of the Union Address and accreditation.* Retrieved from http://www.chea.org/Government/FedUpdate/CHEA_FU29.html

Evans, N. J., & Reason, R. D. (2001). Guiding principles: A review and analysis of student affairs philosophical statements. *Journal of College Student Development, 42,* 359–377.

Hart Research Associates. (2013). *It takes more than a major: Employer priorities for college learning and student success.* Retrieved from http://www.aacu.org/leap/documents/2013_EmployerSurvey.pdf

Huba, M. E. & Freed, J. E. (2000). Learner-centered assessment on college campuses: Shifting the focus from teaching to learning. Boston, MA: Allyn and Bacon.

Keeling, R. P., and Associates (Eds.). (2004). *Learning reconsidered: A campus-wide focus on the student experience.* Washington, DC: National Association of Student Personnel Administrators & American College Personnel Association.

Kuk, L., Cobb, B., & Forrest, C. (2007). Perceptions of competencies of entry-level practitioners in student affairs. *NASPA Journal, 44,* 664–691.

Lumina Foundation. (2013, February 5). *Recent Gallup/Lumina Foundation poll reveals need for higher ed redesign.* Retrieved from http://www.luminafoundation.org/newsroom/news_releases/2013-02-05.html

Northeastern University. (2013, September 17). *Innovation imperative: Enhancing higher education outcomes public opinion survey results.* Retrieved from http://www.northeastern.edu/innovationsurvey/pdfs/Northeastern_University_Innovation_Imperative_Higher_Ed_Outcomes_Poll_Deck_FINAL_Delivered.pdf

Reason, R. D., & Broido, E. M. (2010). Philosophies and values. In J. H. Schuh, S. R. Jones, S. R. Harper, & Associates (Eds.), *Student services: A handbook for the profession* (5th ed. pp. 80–95). San Francisco, CA: Jossey-Bass.

Scholarships.com. (2014). *Rick Perry pushes $10,000 college degree.* Retrieved from https://www.scholarships.com/about-us/press-releases/rick-perry-pushes-10000-college-degree/

Schuh, J. H., & Gansemer-Topf, A. (2010). *The role of student affairs in student learning assessment.* Urbana, IL: University of Illinois–Indiana University & National Institute for Learning Outcomes Assessment. Retrieved from http://learningoutcomesassessment.org/occasionalpaperseven.htm#OP1PaperAbstract

Torres, V., & Walbert, J. (2010). *Updates—The future of student affairs. Final report of the Task Force on the Future of Student Affairs.* Retrieved from http://www.naspa.org/images/uploads/main/Task_Force_Student_Affairs_2010_Report.pdf

Upcraft, M. L., and Schuh, J. H. (1996). *Assessment in student affairs.* San Francisco, CA: Jossey-Bass.

2

TENET TWO: COMMIT TO STUDENT LEARNING AS A PRIMARY FOCUS

James P. Barber

SSAO's Perspective

Barbara Henley

For over 15 years, I have been reciting the phrases "Student learning and assessment" and "Every student affairs department must have at least one learning goal/objective with an assessment component." I have announced incessantly to my associate vice chancellors (AVCs) that we needed to focus on student learning and assess what we were doing for accountability purposes, to demonstrate we were making a difference with our students, and to prepare for the university's accreditation. Using as many venues as possible, I repeated this information at our weekly staff meetings; I referred to my undergraduate Education 101 course where I learned to write measurable learning objectives using Bloom's (1956) taxonomy; and, for a few years, the student learning and assessment theme was interwoven strategically into our annual fall kickoffs and our annual end-of-the-year award programs. Was anyone listening? A few were; however, many student affairs colleagues in our division appeared overwhelmed by the mere idea. We had more work to do.

Subsequently, I hired a part-time coordinator to assist with assessment. Annually, multiple staff development workshops and a certificate of professional development series were planned under the leadership of AVCs and offered to all members of student affairs. Faculty members from departments of higher education were invited often to be our featured speakers. A module on student learning and assessment was incorporated into our orientation for all new staff members. A student affairs assessment committee was appointed, composed of a chairperson and members who had a background in and familiarity with

22

learning and assessment. One of the goals of the committee was to assist our directors and staff with planning and assessing their programs and services. Although the committee was instrumental in conducting divisional-level assessment projects to demonstrate learning, change was slow at the departmental level.

Many staff continued to struggle with student learning and assessment. Some told me they were unsure about how to measure learning, whereas others told me there were no good instruments available for conducting their assessments. To begin to address the issues, we discussed asking students what they had learned as a result of their participation in our services and programs, and we discussed the use of pre- and posttests to determine if anything had been learned.

After hiring a full-time assessment director and filling positions with staff and leadership who had completed higher education and student affairs preparation programs, we are now beginning to advance our student learning and assessment agenda. There is much discussion currently about what we believe students need to learn, the learning outcomes we expect, the programs and services needed to achieve the outcomes, and how we will assess learning and outcomes. We have come a long way. The journey is not complete, but collectively we agree on the destination, and we will reach it.

The tenet "student learning as the core of assessment" is important. After all, we are members of the academy, a learning organization, and we work in a learning environment. The faculty teaches and assesses student learning. As student affairs educators, we must ensure that the students participating in our programs and services outside the classroom are learning through the use of our course materials such as student codes of conduct, workbooks for various workshops, and instructional videos, to name a few. Moreover, our practice and adherence to student learning as the core of assessment enhances our centrality to the academic mission and our credibility as educators. I am reminded how important it is for us to be ready for reaccreditation visits every 10 years. In addition, it is critical to have the data as a result of assessment to demonstrate we are making a difference during, what has become for some of us, annual budget reduction cycles due to recalcitrant economic challenges.

The role of the senior student affairs officer (SSAO) is vital to the success of implementing student learning and assessment. It is important that the SSAO set the tone and emphasize the importance of student learning and assessment. The SSAO must "walk the talk" through the recruitment and employment of an assessment director to lead the initiative, the appointment of an assessment committee to bring different departments together to create energy and synergy around assessment initiatives, the provision of staff and professional development opportunities, and the furnishing of human and fiscal resources for student learning and assessment to occur.

SSAOs are likely to encounter problems. In my attempts to implement the tenet of student learning as the core of assessment, many challenges were faced. One early discovery was that I was asking members of our division to focus on student learning and assessment, and not all of them had backgrounds in edu-

cation or exposure to graduate-level higher education or student affairs prepa-
ration programs. The University of Illinois at Chicago (UIC) did not have
graduate programs in these areas to which I could turn for assistance or refer
my student affairs colleagues. Some of my colleagues simply were not prepared to
conduct assessment; others struggled with modes and instruments of assessment.

I began by identifying ourselves as "student affairs educators." My accompa-
nying message was that the students we serve must learn from their interactions
with us and our programs and services. I announced on multiple occasions and
in multiple venues the importance of student affairs as a learning organization
or a learning laboratory for students and that assessment data were needed to
demonstrate our significance and improve our programs accordingly. I hired
a student affairs and assessment educator to help deliver the message, to pro-
vide the tools through our staff and professional development programs, and to
advance our student learning and assessment agenda. I charged every depart-
ment with having at least one learning objective with an assessment component.
Collectively, the strategies are working.

The UIC student affairs mission is derived from the institutional mis-
sion. It does not and cannot stand alone. It is heresy for us to work outside
the institutional mission, and if we did, it would result in confusion for our
students and raise questions about our work. We must work in collaboration
with our academic affairs colleagues and others to promote and assess student
learning and assessment throughout the academy.

Student Learning and Student Affairs Assessment

The cries for assessment have never been louder in higher education. Ask
any senior administrator in academic affairs or student affairs when the next
regional accreditation visit is scheduled and you are likely to get a quick
answer. Sometimes the pressure for assessment is so strong that college educators can lose sight of the overarching goal of assessment, accreditation, and
other forms of quality assurance programs: documenting student learning.

The publication of *Learning Reconsidered* (Keeling, 2004) brought the
concept of student learning front and center in the field of student affairs.
Subsequent releases including *Learning Reconsidered 2* (Keeling, 2006) and
Assessment Reconsidered (Keeling, Wall, Underhile, & Dungy, 2008) bolstered
the profession's commitment to fostering and improving student learning
experiences. However, it is not enough to create environments or programs
that we believe will advance the learning mission of higher education; we
must implement effective assessment practices to document how our work is
actively promoting college student learning.

I have the privilege to teach a course about higher education assessment
and evaluation for graduate students. I was very intentional about the title of

this course; I wanted to be sure that the focus was squarely on student learning. I decided on "Assessment and Evaluation to Promote College Student Learning." It is a long title, but one that reflects my personal philosophy of assessment and establishes the emphasis on student learning and how assessment can aid in learning. Two predominant questions guide my philosophy of educational assessment: What do we know about student learning? How can we leverage that knowledge to improve learning? In the first chapter, the idea of learning as a reason for conducting assessment is introduced. In this chapter, I explore the role of student learning in the assessment process and discuss prioritizing student learning in assessment.

How College Students Learn

Responsible assessment of student learning begins with an understanding of how people learn (e.g., Ambrose, Bridges, DiPietro, Lovett, & Norman, 2010; Bransford, Brown, Cocking, & National Research Council, 2000). In recent years, fostering student learning has become a central mission of student affairs divisions (Barber & Bureau, 2012; Keeling, 2004). As student affairs professionals focus our work increasingly on student learning, it is essential that we "catch up" on over a century of research on teaching and learning. Most higher education and student affairs preparation programs offer (or require) a course on college student development, exploring the ways in which students grow and change within the college context. Far fewer programs offer a course investigating college student learning. The result is that the majority of professionals trained in traditional graduate preparation programs do not understand how college students learn.

Prior Knowledge and Transfer

Students' prior knowledge matters; they do not arrive at a college or university as a blank slate. Most individuals have at least 17 or 18 years of life experience to draw upon as they enter higher education and routinely transfer learning from their previous experiences to their new contexts. Over a century ago, Thorndike and Woodworth (1901) developed the *identical elements theory* of transfer. They defined this theory by positing that transferring learning from one situation to another was most likely when there were identical or similar elements in the two situations. Judd (1939) challenged the notion that identical elements were necessary to facilitate transfer, proposing instead that *general principles*, defined as broad generalizations of knowledge, were more important for transfer than memorizing specific pieces of information.

Gestalt psychology (Katona, 1940; Wertheimer, 1945/1959) advanced the idea of general principles and offered a third view of transfer of learning, which suggested that learning by *understanding meaning* facilitated transfer better than learning by rote. In the late twentieth century, research on *metacognition*, defined as the knowledge of one's own cognition (thinking), synthesized components of transfer theory from previous generations (Mayer & Wittrock, 1996). Metacognition views transfer as a series of learning processes rather than a single task. The metacognitive transfer approach suggests that transfer is heightened when students have learned specific information that is applicable to a given situation (identical elements), particularly when combined with a broader context of knowledge (general principles). With a holistic, contextual understanding (understanding meaning) of a particular question, problem, or task, a student can then choose among relevant knowledge resources and select his or her best approach.

Metacognitive learning has been linked closely with contemporary models of personal development and provides a nexus for the literatures of college student development and learning (King & Siddiqui, 2011). The evolution of thought on learning transfer strongly supports the notion that students' prior knowledge is extremely relevant to new learning. Simply put, if we as college educators do not open the door to students' prior knowledge, we are sacrificing rich opportunities for learning.

Experiential Learning

Although formal education certainly contributes to college students' knowledge base, experiential learning contributes as well, adding significantly to students' current learning. Student affairs professionals have direct oversight for much of the cocurricular or out-of-the-classroom learning at colleges and universities. Experiential learning may take the form of contemporary practices such as living–learning communities, residence life programming, virtual or computer simulation experiences, service-learning courses, study abroad or away experiences, and leadership in student organizations. Despite the modern sound of these familiar programs, experiential learning has been studied for the better part of a century.

Lewin's (1936) interactionist perspective is familiar to many student affairs professionals due to its inclusion in student development literature. His formula $B = f(P \times E)$ represents the concept that behavior is a function of the interaction between a person and his or her environment. John Dewey's (1938) research also supports the influence of experiential learning. His theory of experience suggested that experiences both inside and outside the formal classroom and curriculum contribute substantially to student learning. In a variety of roles, student affairs professionals serve this progressive purpose of helping students develop, organize, and ultimately make meaning of their experience.

Kolb (1984) is another scholar upon whom student affairs professionals often draw due to his focus on experiential learning common in cocurricular programs. Kolb built upon the work of Lewin, Dewey, and Piaget in developing the experiential learning model. In his model, Kolb identified four different abilities that effective learners need to be effective: concrete experience, reflective observation, abstract conceptualization, and active experimentation.

Integration of Learning

In higher education and student affairs, we are concerned with not only the ability to transfer knowledge from one situation to another and the acquisition of knowledge through experience, but also student ability to *integrate learning* among various sources and contexts. I define this concept as follows:

> Integration of learning is the demonstrated ability to connect, apply, and/or synthesize information coherently from disparate contexts and perspectives, and make use of these new insights in multiple contexts. This includes the ability to connect the domain of ideas and philosophies to the everyday experience, from one field of study or discipline to another, from the past to the present, between campus and community life, from one part to the whole, from the abstract to the concrete, among multiple identity roles—and vice versa. (Barber, 2012, p. 593)

Integration of learning is a familiar concept to those working in student affairs roles. My own interest in student learning originated from my experiences in student affairs advising undergraduate student leaders and watching them link learning experiences across contexts. Some students could integrate learning deftly, whereas others struggled.

Undergraduates use three primary approaches to integrate learning: (a) connection, (b) application, and (c) synthesis. These three ways of integrating differ in degree of complexity. *Connection* is an initial discovery of a similarity between ideas, but beyond the recognition of similarity, the ideas remain distinct. *Application* is the actual use of knowledge or skills learned in one context in another context. The student moves beyond connecting ideas and puts learning into action. Finally, *synthesis* is a creative process in which the individual brings together two or more ideas to form something new. In synthesizing, the student becomes even more deeply involved with the knowledge or skills. Although less experienced students rely heavily on connection and application, as individuals progress in college, they become more adept at using all three approaches to integration in concert (Barber, 2009, 2012, 2014).

In considering strategies for keeping student learning at the center of student affairs assessment, it is useful to shift our collective frame of reference for our profession from an instruction paradigm to a learning paradigm (Barr & Tagg, 1995). Fried and associates (2012) encouraged a view of learning as an integrated process, not limited to academic affairs and the traditional classroom, and positioned student affairs practice as "experiential transformative education" (p. 10). As the student affairs profession begins to move toward a more integrative view of education, in which student affairs professionals are responsible for student learning as opposed to more administrative "student support services" functions, the field faces increased expectations to position student learning as the core of our assessment efforts. Starting with the end in mind—that is, the learning that our programs, resources, and services aim to foster—is vital. Therefore, establishing clear and practical learning outcomes matters.

Drafting Learning Outcomes

Armed with a better understanding of *how* students learn, student affairs professionals can more deeply consider *what* students learn. In assessment of student learning, process matters greatly and establishing clear, measurable learning outcomes is a key initial step. The educational experience or curriculum is then planned with the student learning outcomes in mind, with a focus on how to best facilitate student achievement of the stated outcomes. Only then should the assessment method be considered to find the most effective and efficient way to evaluate whether a student has successfully mastered the outcome(s). In this way, student learning is the starting point in the process, and the curriculum and assessment are aligned to best support students in reaching the outcome.

In drafting student learning outcomes, it is important to be clear, concise, and realistic. Consider the fairy tale "Goldilocks and the Three Bears" when developing learning outcomes. Just as Goldilocks sought out the porridge that was not too hot, not too cold, but just right, educators need to develop learning outcomes that are not so broad that they lose meaning, but also not so specific that they become unattainable for the majority of students. Like Goldilocks, you want to find the balance that is just right.

The ABCD method for writing learning outcomes (Heinich, Molenda, Russell, & Smaldino, 1996) is a practical tool for educators to use in the initial stages of assessment. In this formula, A represents *audience*; in most cases, students participating in a particular experience are the audience for your learning outcome. B is the desired *behavior*, a descriptor of what students are expected to be able to do as a result of participation in the experience. C is the *context* for learning, which could also be termed the *curriculum* or the *condition*; this element describes where you are providing the opportunity for students to learn the desired behavior. Finally, D represents the *degree* to which the behavior is performed. Common examples of the degree include a percentage score on an assignment or ability to perform a task within a specified time limit or in varied contexts. When you put the elements of the formula together, you develop a learning outcome that reads similar to: "As a result of participating in [context], [audience] will be able to [behavior] to a specific [degree.]" For example: As a result of participating in a mock interview with the career center, students will be able to identify one or more questions an employer is likely to ask in a real-life interview. In this sample learning outcome, the audience is "students," the behavior is "identify . . . questions an employer is likely to ask," the context is "a mock interview," and the degree is "one or more questions."

Models for Assessment

Choosing an appropriate framework for your assessment is critical. In this section, I address the role of theories in assessment of student affairs learning activities as well as standards for best practice in the field. There are several theoretical frameworks that are frequently used in student affairs work, and in this chapter I will discuss two: (a) the I-E-O model (Astin, 1993; Astin & Antonio, 2012) and (b) the self-authorship model (Baxter Magolda, 1999; Baxter Magolda & King, 2012). These two models in particular allow student affairs leaders to view how the work of the division impacts the student experience in terms of learning and development and consider what programming and resources should be provided across the experience.

The I-E-O model describes the inputs (I), environments (E), and outputs (O) of education, with a focus on the change between the inputs and outputs; that is, the student characteristics prior to and after participating in a particular educational experience. The self-authorship model is a developmental framework that describes individual growth in three dimensions of development: cognitive, intrapersonal, and interpersonal. The journey toward self-authorship charts a continuum of meaning making in these three domains, moving from externally defined views of knowledge, identity, and relationships to internally derived foundations. These are not mutually exclusive frameworks, and many educators use both, or elements of each, in their work. Next, I describe these two models in greater detail.

I-E-O Model

Alexander Astin first proposed the foundation for the I-E-O model in 1962 as a way to understand the relationship between an institution's input of high-achieving freshmen and output of PhD graduates (Astin, 1962; Astin & Antonio, 2012). He found that the characteristics of incoming students (standardized test scores, GPA, etc.) were highly predictive of how many students would go on to earn a doctorate (Astin, 1962). The I-E-O model provides a simple and logical framework for looking at student learning: Where does the student start, what environmental experiences does the student participate in, and where does the student finish? In Astin's own words (1993), "the basic purpose of the model is to assess the impact of various environmental experiences by determining whether students grow or change differently under varying environmental conditions" (p. 7). The focus is on the impact the college environment has on the student; that is, the change between the input and output (Figure 2.1).

Astin noted that even with excellent information about both the student inputs and outputs, our grasp of the educational process is limited if we do not understand the experiences and curricula that comprise the college environment (Astin & Antonio, 2012). As illustrated in Figure 2.1, the student inputs directly affect both the environment and the outputs. Where you focus on this model may depend on where you work on campus. Those concerned with recruiting and admission see arrow A as primary and want to know more about how students' incoming characteristics might affect school choice or, in other words, how and why different types of students may select different college environments.

Historically, administrators and external audiences have been highly interested in arrow C, the direct relationship between students as they enter and depart the institution. The environmental component is sometimes referred to as a "black box" in understanding the impact of higher

Figure 2.1 The I-E-O Model

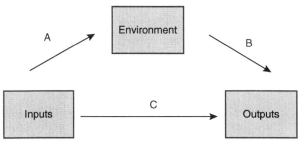

Source: Astin & Antonio, 2012.

education. Researchers know a great deal about the inputs (SAT and ACT score, high school GPA, socioeconomic status) and the outputs (graduation rate, employment statistics, median income), but, often, very little about the experiences that students have between matriculation and graduation. In student affairs assessment, the focus is often on arrow B, the ways in which the environment (including cocurricular programs, residential life, support services, etc.) affects the outputs; in many assessment projects, there is little or no consideration of the inputs.

To return to the earlier example of a mock interview in a campus career center, the inputs may include a student's prior knowledge (previous work, experience interviewing) and program of study. The environment is the practice interview itself, as well as any accompanying feedback, processing, and resulting intervention programs facilitated by professionals in the career center. Finally, the outcome is the student's success in securing a job offer.

Self-Authorship Model

The self-authorship model is a developmental framework that can be useful in assessing how students grow and change over time. Grounded in the constructive–developmental approach, the self-authorship model asserts that meaning making is individually constructed by people in context (i.e., constructivism), and evolves into more complex forms over time (i.e., developmentalism). Self-authorship has three dimensions: (a) cognitive or epistemological, focused on how a person sees knowledge and the world around him or her; (b) intrapersonal, focused on how an individual sees himself or herself; and (c) interpersonal, focused on how someone views relationships with others (Baxter Magolda, 1999). Using the self-authorship model as an assessment framework may be particularly attractive to student affairs educators because it allows for exploration of how students are learning holistically, taking into consideration these three domains of cognition, identity, and relationships (Figure 2.2).

The journey toward self-authorship is individual development along a continuum through three main meaning-making structures: (a) external meaning making, (b) a transitional crossroads phase, and (c) internal meaning making. These three structures are further subdivided into 10 positions on the continuum, describing nuanced ways of thinking (Baxter Magolda & King, 2012). Although there is an overall developmental trajectory from a reliance on external frameworks to creating internal foundations for meaning making, the journey along this continuum is not linear. The developmental path may differ for each individual, and the

Figure 2.2 Self-Authorship Model

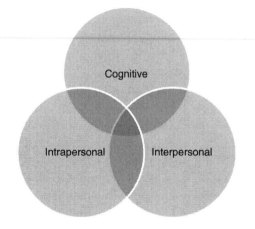

progression toward self-authorship in the three domains is better represented by a helix rather than a straight line (Baxter Magolda and King,
2012).

Due to its developmental nature, the self-authorship model can
be a practical framework for both developing and assessing learning
outcomes. Many of the complexities of meaning making necessary for self-
authorship are also characteristic of metacognition, including the benefits
of deep reflection and personal agency (King & Siddiqui, 2011). The self-
authorship model has been used to assess specific outcomes relevant to
student affairs education, such as intercultural maturity (King & Baxter
Magolda, 2005), as well as to develop and assess the outcomes of multiyear curricula, including the Miami University Honors Program (Taylor &
Haynes, 2008).

Regarding the career center mock interview in terms of the self-
authorship model, student affairs educators would consider the perspectives
of students at different developmental levels. For example, a first-year student visiting the center for the first time to prepare for a summer internship
interview may need initial exposure to the interview process, coaching on
appropriate attire, and tips on eye contact and posture. A graduating senior
with previous interview experience may need more assistance discussing how
his or her field of study aligns with the intended employer and negotiating
salary and benefits. Student affairs educators can apply the three dimensions
of development in this case as well, considering how the student views the
world and employment landscape around him or her (cognitive), himself or
herself as a candidate (intrapersonal), and the relationship with the inter-
viewer/potential employer (interpersonal).

Standards and Frameworks for Assessing Student Learning

In addition to the theoretical models reviewed previously, professional standards and frameworks in higher education and student affairs can be excellent resources for assessing student learning. The Degree Qualifications Profile (DQP) (Adelman, Ewell, Gaston, & Geary Schneider, 2014), the Valid Assessment of Learning in Undergraduate Education (VALUE) rubrics (Association of American Colleges and Universities [AAC&U], 2009), and the Council for the Advancement of Standards in Higher Education (CAS) *Professional Standards for Higher Education* (CAS, 2012) are three valuable tools for assessment.

The DQP is the broadest of the three and the only framework developed to define the student learning expected from various academic degrees. The DQP offers baseline criteria for what students should know and be able to do to earn associate's, bachelor's, and master's degrees, regardless of major and field of study (Adelman et al., 2014). The DQP can serve as a useful benchmarking tool for student affairs educators who also work with a broad array of students across majors and disciplines. In addition, student affairs leaders can use this model to develop a cocurricular framework for the division that complements degree-level outcomes. The DQP and resources on implementation can be found online for free (www .degreeprofile.org).

The AAC&U, which focuses on liberal learning at the undergraduate level, has developed a series of 16 rubrics for assessing student learning, based on the organization's "Essential Learning Outcomes" first described in *College Learning for the New Global Century* (AAC&U, 2007). Collectively titled the VALUE rubrics, they were created as part of an initiative to develop direct assessments of student learning that would provide authentic and convincing evidence of student learning. The VALUE rubrics were first released in 2009 and are available for free (www.aacu.org/VALUE/rubrics).

The tenets found within the CAS *Professional Standards for Higher Education* (CAS, 2012) stand out as the most comprehensive collection of standards available for student affairs, student services, and student development. The CAS standards are a long-held approach to developing higher education programs, in use by higher education professionals for over 35 years. The standards are centered on student learning outcomes organized into six broad domains, many of which draw upon the theories of learning and development discussed previously: (a) knowledge acquisition, construction, integration, and application; (b) cognitive complexity; (c) intrapersonal development; (d) interpersonal competence; (e) humanitarianism and civic engagement; and (f) practical competence.

CAS (2012) currently offers standards and guidelines for 44 different functional areas in higher education and student affairs; examples include academic advising programs, career services, fraternity/sorority advising programs, service-learning programs, and undergraduate research programs. In addition to the standards themselves, each area has an accompanying self-assessment guide, which provides institutions with a practical map for assessing program effectiveness based on the CAS standards.

The SSAO Role: Applying Frameworks to Assess Learning in Student Affairs

For effective assessment of student learning, student affairs leaders must connect the frameworks and standards with assessment of student learning on campus. As discussed earlier in this chapter, the process matters. Start with an understanding of how people learn and then use that knowledge to draft clear learning outcomes. Next, choose the assessment methods that would be best at documenting the learning in a particular program or environment. However, the process does not end with the data collection. Too often, information is gathered to satisfy external accreditors or stakeholders, only to be archived in a binder or computer folder once the report is submitted. Using most of these frameworks, student affairs educators can not only assess the extent to which experiences have helped students move to one stage, but also assist in developing strategies to move to the next stage or context.

Sharing the findings of assessment is essential for transparent leadership in higher education, and it is important to develop a clear plan to disseminate findings regularly to multiple constituencies, including parents, legislators, alumni, faculty/staff, and of course the students themselves. Although reporting on progress is an important part of assessment work, it is not the end goal. Unless we as educators are using the data to promote student learning, we are not realizing the full potential of assessment.

Conclusion

This chapter explores a number of frameworks and resources that can assist student affairs professionals in meaningful assessment of student learning. In planning assessment efforts, educators must keep the process in mind. We begin with thoughtful consideration of the intended learning outcomes, develop strong environments in which learning can flourish, collect authentic evidence of student learning, and then are intentional about closing the cycle by using the knowledge gained to improve the student learning experience. Most importantly, educators need to understand *how* students learn in order to effectively assess learning and create educational experiences that work. Assessment practice firmly grounded in learning theory and aggressively focused on improving student learning will lead to greater success in ultimately achieving learning outcomes.

It is vital to understand why assessment is important and to uncover the frameworks behind student affairs practices that encourage learning. The next section focuses on how divisional leadership is demonstrated and culture is changed by SSAOs securing staff buy-in: Garrison Duncan and Holmes examine how to get people invested in this idea that assessment in student affairs practice matters.

References

Adelman, C., Ewell, P., Gaston, P., & Geary Schneider, C. (2014). *The Degree Qualifications Profile 2.0: Defining U.S. degrees through demonstration and documentation of college learning.* Retrieved from http://www.luminafoundation.org/publications/DQP/DQP2.0-draft.pdf

Ambrose, S. A., Bridges, M. W., DiPietro, M., Lovett, M. C., & Norman, M. K. (2010). *How learning works: Seven research-based principles for smart teaching.* San Francisco, CA: Jossey-Bass.

Association of American Colleges and Universities. (2007). *College learning for the new global century.* Retrieved from http://www.aacu.org/leap/documents/GlobalCentury_final.pdf

Association of American Colleges and Universities. (2009). *VALUE rubrics.* Retrieved from http://www.aacu.org/VALUE/rubrics/

Astin, A. (1962). "Productivity" of undergraduate institutions. *Science, 136*(3511), 129–135. Retrieved from http://www.jstor.org/stable/1708437

Astin, A. (1993). *What matters in college? Four critical years revisited.* San Francisco, CA: Jossey-Bass.

Astin, A. W., & Antonio, A. L. (2012). *Assessment for excellence: The philosophy and practice of assessment and evaluation in higher education* (2nd ed.). Lanham, MD: Rowman & Littlefield.

Barber, J. P. (2009). Integration of learning: Meaning making for undergraduates through connection, application, and synthesis (N. 3354010). Dissertation Abstracts International database.

Barber, J. P. (2012). Integration of learning: A grounded theory analysis of college students' learning. *American Educational Research Journal, 49*(3), 590–617. doi: 10.3102/0002831212437854

Barber, J. P. (2014). Integration of learning model: How college students integrate learning [Special Section]. *New Directions for Higher Education, 2014*(165), 1–7. doi: 10.1002/he.20079

Barber, J. P., & Bureau, D. (2012). Coming into focus: Positioning student learning from *The Student Personnel Point of View* to today. In K. M. Boyle, J. W. Lowery, & J. A. Mueller (Eds.), *Reflections on the 75th anniversary of* The Student Personnel Point of View (pp. 35–40). Washington, DC: American College Personnel Association & College Student Educators International.

Barr, R. B., & Tagg, J. (1995). From teaching to learning: A new paradigm for undergraduate education. *Change: The Magazine of Higher Learning, 27*(6), 12–25. Retrieved from http://www.jstor.org.proxy.wm.edu/stable/40165284

Baxter Magolda, M. B. (1999). *Creating contexts for learning and self-authorship: Constructive-developmental pedagogy.* Nashville, TN: Vanderbilt University Press.

Baxter Magolda, M. B., & King, P. M. (2012). Assessing meaning making and self-authorship: Theory, research, and application [Monograph]. *ASHE Higher Education Report Series, 38*(3). San Francisco, CA: Jossey-Bass. doi: 10.1002/aehe.20003

Bloom, B. S. (Ed.). (1956). *Taxonomy of educational objectives: The classification of educational goals. Handbook I: Cognitive domain.* New York, NY: David McKay.

Bransford, J., Brown, A. L., Cocking, R. R., & National Research Council (U.S.). (2000). *How people learn: Brain, mind, experience, and school.* Washington, DC: National Academies Press.

Council for the Advancement of Standards. (2012). *CAS professional standards for higher education* (9th ed.). Washington, DC: Author.

Dewey, J. (1938). *Experience and education.* New York, NY: Collier Books.

Fried, J., & Associates. (2012). *Transformative learning through engagement: Student affairs practice as experiential pedagogy.* Sterling, VA: Stylus.

Heinich, R., Molenda, M., Russell, J. D., & Smaldino, S. E. (1996). *Instructional media and technologies for learning.* Englewood Cliffs, NJ: Merrill.

Judd, C. H. (1939). *Educational psychology.* New York, NY: Houghton Mifflin.

Katona, G. (1940). *Organizing and memorizing: Studies in the psychology of learning and teaching.* New York, NY: Hafner.

Keeling, R. P. (Ed.). (2004). *Learning reconsidered: A campus-wide focus on student experience.* Washington, DC: American College Personnel Association & National Association of Student Personnel Administrators.

Keeling, R. P. (Ed.). (2006). *Learning reconsidered 2: Implementing a campus-wide focus on the student experience.* Washington, DC: American College Personnel Association, Association of College and University Housing Officers-International, Association of College Unions-International, National Academic Advising Association, National Association for Campus Activities, National Association of Student Personnel Administrators, & National Intramural-Recreational Sports Association.

Keeling, R. P., Wall, A. F., Underhile, R., & Dungy, G. J. (2008). *Assessment reconsidered: Institutional effectiveness for student success.* Washington, DC: International Center for Student Success and Institutional Accountability.

King, P. M., & Baxter Magolda, M. B. (2005). A developmental model of inter-cultural maturity. *Journal of College Student Development, 46*(6), 571–592. doi:10.1353/csd.2005.0060

King, P. M., & Siddiqui, R. (2011). Self-authorship and metacognition: Related constructs for understanding college student learning and development. In C. Hoare (Ed.), *The Oxford handbook of reciprocal adult development and learning* (pp. 113–131). New York, NY: Oxford University Press.

Kolb, D. A. (1984). *Experiential learning: Experience as the source of learning and development.* Englewood Cliffs, NJ: Prentice Hall.

Lewin, K. (1936). *Principles of topological psychology.* New York, NY: McGraw-Hill.

Mayer, R. E., & Wittrock, M. C. (1996). Problem-solving transfer. In D. C. Berliner & R. C. Calfee (Eds.). *Handbook of educational psychology* (pp. 47–62). New York, NY: Macmillan.

Taylor, K., & Haynes, C. (2008). A framework for intentionally fostering student learning. *About Campus, 13*(5), 2–11. doi:10.1002/abc.265

Thorndike, E. L., & Woodworth, R. S. (1901). The influence of improvement in one mental function upon the efficiency of other functions. *Psychological Review, 8*, 247–261.

Wertheimer, M. (1945/1959). *Productive thinking.* New York, NY: Harper.

PART TWO

DIVISION LEADERSHIP AND CULTURE

"The only thing of real importance that leaders do is to create and manage culture. If you do not manage culture, it manages you, and you may not even be aware of the extent to which this is happening."

Edgar Schein, *Organizational Culture and Leadership*, 2010

"Culture does not change because we desire to change it. Culture changes when the organization is transformed; the culture reflects the realities of people working together every day."

Frances Hesselbein, "The Key to Cultural Transformation," *Leader to Leader*, Spring, 1999

Why does culture matter? This book is distinctive in that we are discussing culture change and developing sound assessment practices as simultaneous processes. These two go hand in hand but are rarely explored in concert with each other. We discuss culture first, as we believe it is the foundation that allows assessment to begin to take hold and ultimately transform the division into a community of practitioners who can utilize evidence to make decisions. This section of the book is designed to clarify the aspects of division culture in which leaders must inspire change and then develop and use management tools to ensure practices are reinforced and sustained in the culture.

3

TENET THREE: LAY THE FOUNDATION FOR A SUSTAINABLE ASSESSMENT CULTURE

Amber Garrison Duncan and Robin H. Holmes

SSAO's Perspective

Robin H. Holmes

Change is hard. When we are faced with doing something differently, even if doing so has positive implications, our natural reaction is to resist in some way. Educating and then influencing a division to utilize assessment as a necessary tool for overall success is a big task and can be a daunting change. It becomes even more complicated when one considers the tendency toward positive impression management to which we all are subject ("My director wants me to be excited about assessment, so I will be!"). Not surprisingly, if something appears difficult, new, ill defined, threatening, or time consuming, we will be less than enthusiastic about embracing it.

Although "talk" about building a culture of assessment has been ratcheting up for over a decade (Slager & Oaks, 2013), a general scan of the literature still demonstrates more "how to think about doing it" than great examples of "just doing it." Why is that the case? Because as with anything that is difficult, we resist it. As leaders we often have to identify the common defenses that are put up in response to assessment.

Setting the vision, mission, and direction for the division is the main role of the chief student affairs officer. In order to move toward a culture of assessment, all division personnel must understand the significance and importance of building a culture of assessment throughout the division. The senior student affairs officer (SSAO) must model data-based decision making and demonstrate a vested interest in knowing how the various programs, services, and learning opportunities offered throughout the division are affecting students (Busby & Gonzalez Robinson, 2012).

As the SSAO, the first thing to do is to reflect on the messages, direction, communication, and incentives that you are providing as the leader of the division. Using education and influence, leaders can create a culture shift that will support assessment.

Student Affairs Values: Personalizing Why Culture Change Is Vital

Previous chapters have outlined the imperative for assessment in student affairs and how student learning has become a focus of such assessments. Understanding the rationale is one thing, but it's time to think about how leaders move an entire division of practitioners to act on behalf of the plans. Time and experience have taught us that implementing practices that support assessment and evidence-based decision making requires a shift in the culture of the division (Love & Estanek, 2004; Sandeen & Barr, 2006). This is not just about training professionals how to do a job; this is about creating a community of practice where people share in a process of learning new knowledge and skills. It is about using evidence for improvement and finding new ways to work in order to deliver positive student outcomes and overall success. As reflected in the SSAO testimony, this requires leadership from the SSAO by way of setting a tone, telling a compelling story, facilitating dialogue, providing motivation, and examining every activity to ensure it moves the division toward a culture that supports assessment and learning.

In order to change culture, we have to start with values, beliefs, and assumptions. A brief review of seminal documents in the field can serve as the cornerstone for determining what values, beliefs, and assumptions professionals in student affairs should enact (Evans & Reason, 2001; Reason & Broido, 2010). Our values call for us to be agents of change on behalf of students; we are tasked with championing a student-centered, learning-based experience (Bureau, 2011). Regardless of the functional area—orientation, conduct, activities, or recreation—we are all in the business of education and as such we must take seriously our role as educators. It is these values on which we can rest our reputation. The values of our field unite us as practitioners. Values reflect why an organization exists and can be a compelling launching pad for SSAOs trying to sell their division on assessment.

At many institutions, the assessment of student learning efforts is primarily focused on students' in-class activities. However, to be successful, students must be able to demonstrate not only what they know, but also what they are able to do. This challenges traditional notions of teaching and has opened the door for student affairs to assess and validate outside-the-classroom learning experiences that facilitate applied learning. The commitment of the student affairs profession to include the out-of-classroom experience is more important than ever if students are to achieve a quality education that prepares them for a twenty-first-century economy. It also positions us as educators who must live the values of our field.

It is critical for every professional to facilitate and assess student development and learning in order for students to realize the benefits of a degree. At the same time, we must use these results to understand where we are successful and where we need to find ways to improve learning experiences in the future. Again, this requires professionals on a campus to see themselves as a community of practitioners who embrace the role of educator and seek to continually improve the student experience on the basis of evidence. This shift in culture starts with why we are here and what we believe guides our work. However, even with the best intentions there are occasions when professionals state belief in these values but have a hard time taking action on them. This lack of congruence between values and practices occurs for many reasons. In the next section we look at some of the most common arguments that demonstrate incongruence and how they may be countered.

Change the Conversation

It is important to make use of the influence of the SSAO role to begin to respond to barriers and change the conversation. Here we have outlined common arguments by professionals as reasons for not engaging in assessment. If leaders allow these comments to go without response, the rhetoric will be seen as acceptable and the culture will not change. When faced with this resistance, we offer suggestions on how to reframe the conversation in a way that supports a culture of assessment.

1. *I'm too busy.*
   This statement is probably the most persistent and widely held belief that stands in the way of culture change. Professionals must work tirelessly and often keep late hours, responding to the multitude of campus emergencies as well as the constantly changing needs of students. It can feel like we are all literally running from one issue to another. It is not surprising, then, to see strategic planning, assessing, and creating learning outcomes at the bottom of our list of activities as we respond to the most recent emergency or crisis.

However, this statement also shows that most professionals view assessment as something else to put on the checklist. It is much easier to just do what we know how to do over and over. Then, when the next best practice in the field emerges, we simply add it to the plate without considering the impact on resources (e.g., time, money, people). By contrast, in a culture of assessment, the focus shifts to how to work smarter, not harder, and to how to get the most from the resources available. Professionals are often supporting too many programs and services because they don't know which ones actually accomplish the goals of the division. Decisions about which programs to maintain are difficult to make when there is no evidence supporting outcomes. In a culture of assessment, as it becomes clear what works, decisions about where to spend money and what to eliminate become easier. In the end, knowing exactly where to focus resources will make to-do lists shorter, so we can maximize budgets and ensure better results.

2. *I wasn't trained to do assessment.*
   The need for outcome-based assessment has been clearly broadcasted to student affairs professionals, but many practitioners do not feel adequately prepared to answer this call, nor have they had much experience with assessment (Slager & Oaks, 2013). By focusing on creating a community of practice, where everyone is a learner, we provide space for people to acknowledge what they may need to develop in order to contribute to assessment efforts. It is also important to recognize that professionals will bring different levels of skills and knowledge about assessment. As a longtime SSAO, you may have never been tasked with practicing assessment, whereas newer professionals likely received specific training in their graduate preparation programs. Midlevel professionals are often bogged down as they manage both up and down the organization. The goal should focus on developing the confidence that each staff member can be successful with assessment and prioritize the use of evidence as they go about making decisions at each level of the organization.

3. *I might lose my job.*
   Feelings of inadequacy are often tied to a worry that the results of assessment will not be as described or hoped. Specific examples of fears resulting from poor assessment results include different levels of uncertainty. What if living in the residence hall does not impact retention and graduation rates? What if bystander intervention training does not result in a demonstrable change in student interventions when inappropriate behaviors are present? If the results do not

support positive outcomes for my program, will I lose my funding? Will I no longer have a job?

These are just some of the fears that have been articulated by staff as they have been asked to think about assessing what they are doing. In order to address these fears, we have to understand that failure is acceptable. There is the very real possibility we may find that what we are doing is *not* making the difference we have believed in and based our programs on. In a community of practice, instead of blaming or judging, we turn to assessing what caused the intervention to fail and then use the evidence to change. Thus, we reinforce the value of evidence and reward the practitioner for engaging in the process regardless of outcome. The practitioner's responsibility is to have a willingness to experiment, to learn and find practices that do deliver on intended outcomes for students.

4. *If I wanted to do research, I would have become a faculty member.*
The ability to articulate the difference between assessment and research is important to being able to respond and reframe this statement. Research is often assumed to be the same as assessment because the methods of collecting data and information are often similar, but there is a difference in each activity's use of data that must be distinguished. As described in Chapter 1, the purpose of research is to test theoretical concepts and create new knowledge that can be used broadly. In campus-based assessment, practitioners use as much rigor as possible in a practical setting to gather evidence and inform better practice and policy. Again, if we are creating a community of practice that honors continuous improvement, then data must be collected in order to understand where and how to improve.

The ability to influence attitudes and perceptions about assessment and the role of assessment for staff is critical for creating a culture where assessment is valued. Be prepared to explain the "why" behind the expectations that assessments create, being particularly proactive in providing reminders that our role as educator should always be at the center of our work. You will likely be challenged by colleagues who do not believe that assessment is truly valuable. The way you talk about assessment and prioritize it in every way eliminates the space where disbelief and fear can set in. For this reason it is also very important that both success and failure in terms of program success are expected and rewarded; professional worth is determined by innovation and finding what works, rather than by only reporting positive outcomes.

Committing to Culture Change

Using one's influence as a senior leader in a division of student affairs to change the conversation and support beliefs and attitudes that are conducive to assessment is the first step in developing a culture of assessment. The second step is to foster behaviors to realize the creation of a culture of assessment. There are four ways that a culture of assessment can be fostered: demonstrating commitment, being consistent, making connections with and for staff, and communicating the message well.

Commitment

It is important to demonstrate commitment to assessment by allocating resources (time, money, and people) to assessment. Start somewhere, even if it is just a small amount of money or a quarter of a person's time, because allocating money and designating leadership for assessment sends a clear message that these efforts are important. The evolution at the University of Oregon began with a commitment outlined in the division strategic plan (studentlife .uoregon.edu/strategic-plan). This led to the creation of an implementation committee that defined what was needed to establish assessment practices and policies within the division. The committee recommended that the division assign a full-time person dedicated to leading assessment. Although that was not possible right away, a small budget and a half-time staff member were assigned. Within two years, a full-time assessment professional was in place along with an emerging assessment culture. In times of tight budgets, many divisions start out by creating a committee to share leadership responsibilities or appointing someone on a part-time basis, steps that quickly foster support for further efforts and build the case for why a division needs someone full-time to focus on assessment.

Committing to assessment also means committing to the education and development of staff. A person or group should be charged with providing professional development for staff on assessment. On some campuses, the assessment committee provides training or a delegated student affairs human resources officer is responsible for training. Before requiring staff to conduct assessment, it is always best to review the knowledge and skills of professionals who are slated to engage in assessment. That review may reveal that knowledge and skills are low. Accordingly, before appointing a training committee you may need to cultivate and train prospective members so they can then provide education across the division. Make use of webinars and campus faculty who can reach a larger number of people for less money. Staff can also be directed to functional area resources for specific examples of what assessment can look like—for example, in housing or leadership programs.

The more that staff feel they have opportunities to support and engage in assessment, the more likely they are to follow through.

In addition to education and development, there is a wide variety of tools that can expand the capacity of the division to access, collect, analyze, and use evidence. Expecting a verbal charge to change behavior is not a realistic expectation and it is nearly impossible for staff to go from novice to expert in assessment. There are many resources available from the field that can be built upon; some are free and some cost money. Commit to investing in tools that create systemic reinforcement of assessment so staff need not to create something new at each step in the assessment process. The use of these tools can create small wins and deepen commitment as staff begin to see that they actually can do assessment. These tools include online data-collection tools (i.e., CampusLabs, Qualtrics), plug-and-play assessment instruments (i.e., AAC&U VALUE rubrics), report templates, and access to project consultation.

Last but not least, in order to demonstrate commitment, give permission. It sounds simple, but be vocal about permission to spend time on assessment instead of something else, to challenge the status quo, to take risks, and to fail. We have found that staff members are sometimes afraid to try something new or stop doing something tried and true because they think it will reflect negatively on them when, in reality, that is often not the case. Be clear about what is essential or a top priority for the division and then open up time and space for staff to have permission to pause or stop a program so they can try something new or fine-tune their assessment process. Expecting staff to add assessment on to what they are currently doing is how it quickly becomes an "add-on" rather a part of best practice. Then make sure you practice what you preach. If the SSAO and members of the senior leadership team do not purposefully dedicate time and resources to make assessment a priority in the division, there is a good chance that staff will neither prioritize assessment nor change what they are doing on a day-to-day basis.

Consistency

As we know, changing behaviors takes consistency until it becomes a habit. Through planning, explained in Chapter 8, we can ensure priorities are clear and develop approaches to ensure that assessment takes place consistently. SSAOs must make sure assessment and evidence are a part of every conversation, every decision. Using SSAO Bingham's question "How do I know?" from Chapter 1 when responding to assertions or ideas, the most important thing you can do as the SSAO is to hold the line of consistency so that evidence-based decision making and practices become the norm.

Connection

To have a culture means that there is connection among people; the relationships and connections that will sustain a culture should be both internal to the division and extend outward into the institution and the profession. Senior leaders must work diligently to reinforce that staff are a community of practitioners who are there to support each other. Something simple created at the University of Oregon was a yearly assessment summit where staff shared their assessment projects and learned new skills from each other. The summit created "small wins" for professionals as they were able to see that they belonged to a community that valued assessment and were able to contribute to this community. Public forums can also demonstrate that a community of practice that values assessment is actively working to improve interventions and services on behalf of students, opening the door for honest conversations and the opportunity to "fail forward" where failure is a learning opportunity.

It is also important to reinforce culture by connecting student affairs assessment efforts to others within the institution. Forging partnerships with institutional research, human subjects, undergraduate studies, graduate schools, and libraries—anyone doing student learning assessment—connects the division to the larger university mission and goals. Expansion of the student affairs community opens up additional resources for the division to take advantage of training and collaborate on projects, allowing staff to demonstrate their value as educators to the entire campus community.

Lastly, encourage and support staff in joining professional endeavors in the field that help them feel connected to the larger mission and purpose of student affairs. Many, if not all, professional associations now have assessment resources available. The use of evidence in decision making is something that can and should be discussed in professional settings. This can also be achieved by referring to professional competencies (i.e., ACPA/ NASPA Professional Competency Areas for Student Affairs Practitioners) and providing opportunities to connect with training and experiences that support staff development and confidence in these competencies.

Communication

The key to any good relationship is communication. Create opportunities to communicate about assessment efforts within the division. We have already outlined how important rhetoric and changing the conversation is to creating a culture of assessment. It should be mentioned again how important it is for the division to communicate the importance of creating student-centered, learning-based experiences for students. Everyone is an educator and this should be communicated in division materials and reinforced in communications with staff. If you have a marketing professional or use campus marketing support, have them review every piece of communications material to make sure the message is clearly transmitted.

In addition, the division must demonstrate a willingness to communicate openly about assessment and improvement. This requires a level of transparency that can sometimes be difficult to implement as it can create vulnerability and fear. At the University of Oregon, we brought the National Institute for Learning Outcomes assessment transparency framework to the division as the model for how to create transparency and communicate our work. Projects were posted online, and executive summaries of results were shared. Although only a beginning, the transparency framework created a road map for how to best communicate evidence of student success and find ways in which continuous improvements could be made. The authors of Chapter 10 discuss marketing campaigns where divisions have let subjects know how they have improved based on student feedback. This is yet another way to show that the division consistently assesses its work and makes every effort to produce evidence-based improvements.

Conclusion

We have outlined some specific steps that will get you on the road to culture change. Again, all the plans in the world can be in place, but without a culture shift the plans will be useless. Once you start these initial steps, you will need to do more to make specific changes in division processes and procedures. The following chapters provide additional insights on ways to realize the culture change for which you have diligently laid the foundation. These insights include strategies to continue to engage staff in culture change via supervision and performance evaluation, professional development, budget allocations, and job descriptions. Chapter 4 explores ways to engage staff in assessment and Chapter 5 outlines ways to reinforce culture by insisting on accountability and offering rewards. In Chapter 6, you will see the four Cs (commitment, consistency, connection, and communication) again as ways to anchor the newly created culture and sustain it over time.

References

Bureau, D. A. (2011). *"Making them my own": Student affairs master's students' socialization to professional values* (Doctoral dissertation). Available from ProQuest Dissertation and Theses database. (UMI No. 3456444).

Busby, K., & Gonzalez Robinson, B. (2012). Developing the leadership team to establish and maintain a culture of evidence in student affairs. In M. M. Culp & G. J. Dungy (Eds.), *Building a culture of evidence in student affairs: A guide for leaders and practitioners* (pp. 35–59). Washington, DC: NASPA.

Evans, N. J., & Reason, R. D. (2001). Guiding principles: A review and analysis of student affairs philosophical statements. *Journal of College Student Development, 42*, 359–377.

Love, P., & Estanek, S. M. (2004). *Rethinking student affairs practice*. San Francisco, CA: Jossey-Bass.

Reason, R. D., & Broido, E. M. (2010). Philosophies and values. In J. H. Schuh, S. R. Jones, S. R. Harper, & Associates (Eds.), *Student services: A handbook for the profession* (5th ed., pp. 80–95). San Francisco, CA: Jossey-Bass.

Sandeen, A., & Barr, M. J. (2006). *Critical issues for student affairs: Challenges and opportunities*. San Francisco, CA: Jossey-Bass.

Slager, E. M., & Oaks, D. A. J. (2013). A coaching model for student affairs assessment. *About Campus, 18*(3), 25–29.

4

TENET FOUR: DEVELOP STRATEGIES TO ENGAGE STAFF IN A COMMITMENT TO ASSESSMENT

Brenda "B" Woods and William D. Schafer

SSAO's Perspective

William D. Schafer

From 2003 through 2014, I served as the senior student affairs officer (SSAO) for the Division of Student Affairs at the Georgia Institute of Technology. Assessment has been and continues to be a priority in direct alignment with the institute's strategic plan goal to "relentlessly pursue institutional effectiveness" and our division's strategic plan goal to "lead the profession of student affairs by advancing innovative programs, services, and staff development in the pursuit of institutional effectiveness." Although our practices are in line with institutional and divisional priorities, ensuring that staff are committed to assessment is not necessarily a done deal.

Assessment is essential for us to continuously improve the quality of our programs and services. It provides us with increased accountability, demonstrates responsibility, impacts student development, and measures our effectiveness. In my experience as the SSAO, creating and sustaining assessment buy-in is an ongoing process. Of course, opportunities to help staff see the value of assessment are always present, particularly as positions in student affairs turn over or other priorities such as responding to the immediate needs of students become first and foremost. It is not a "one-and-done" kind of deal, and ultimately we have to help staff see how assessment can be appropriately added onto their work and eventually integrated into their practice.

51

As the SSAO, I might deliver the charge while my staff works to enact the vision. It is critical that we have assessment data to tell our story in student affairs or others will create the story of what we do, viewed through their own lens. Assessment processes thoughtfully employed with outcomes incorporated into decision making clearly improve our programs and services for students and other campus constituencies. It is also clear from my work at the Georgia Institute of Technology that a full-time director of assessment for a division of student affairs can help educate and encourage division staff to see the value in a solid assessment program, which leads to the buy-in necessary for long-term improvements.

Developing Strategies to Engage Staff in a Commitment to Assessment

Creating and sustaining assessment buy-in is an elusive yet desirable goal among student affairs assessment professionals and SSAOs. Previous chapters have focused on why assessment is important and the typical challenges to assessment culture. This chapter focuses on what must be considered and enacted as an SSAO leads efforts to embed assessment within the DNA of a division.

Know the Campus Culture

Institutions of higher education have their own unique campus culture and climate. In an effort to create and sustain buy-in, it is imperative for staff to have knowledge of campus values and understand how those core values drive assessment initiatives. Buy-in, however, may be challenging depending on the leadership team; the assessment project history at the institution; the degree to which decisions are made based on assessment results; and the assessment-related perceptions among students, faculty, and staff.

In 2013, the National Institute for Learning Outcomes Assessment (NILOA) repeated a 2009 study known among assessment practitioners as "the Provost study" (Baker, Jankowski, Provezis, & Kinzie, 2012). All 2,781 accredited, undergraduate degree-granting two- and four-year public, private, and for-profit institutions in the United States were invited to participate in the study, which achieved a 43% response rate with 1,202 institutions. One notable finding was a negative correlation between faculty at prominent, high-status institutions and their support of and engagement with assessment. At high-ranking institutions, which are among the best colleges in the nation, resistance may be encountered when asked to provide evidence of institutional effectiveness. An arrogant, just-look-at-the-rankings mind-set is likely to impede the collection of required documentation. In preparation for an institution's accreditation reaffirmation, especially at highly selective research institutions, assessment practitioners would be well served to be mindful of the attitudes among some faculty and/or staff about assessment. Awareness of such viewpoints on campus is vital to creating and sustaining assessment buy-in.

But what happens when these cultural attributes are found in student affairs? Culture can be a powerful force; however, attending to problematic culture must be a priority for SSAOs and their staff. As we examine culture as an important consideration in creating buy-in, we must look to the people who are most responsible for the culture within their divisions of student affairs—SSAOs.

Create Systemic and Systematic Assessment Processes

Creating and sustaining assessment buy-in requires assessment to be ongoing, systemic, and systematic. *Systemic assessment* is defined as the interconnectedness among staff, departments within the division, and the division as a whole. In this case, assessment is an essential, integral part of the division. One key to successful buy-in is to help staff understand that their contributions through assessment initiatives reflect how the division values, and the extent to which they themselves value, the importance of measuring our programs, services, and student learning for continuous improvement.

One forum in which culture can be conveyed is through position descriptions. These documents tell potential and current employees the metrics for performance in the position. Ensuring that potential employees understand the importance of assessment begins with placing assessment in the position description and/or in the advertisement for the job, such as the following: "In collaboration with the director and staff in the Student Affairs Office of Assessment, the individual employed in this position will be responsible and held accountable for collecting, analyzing, interpreting, and reporting data for the purpose of improving programs and services. Evidence of assessment will be reviewed biannually by the supervisor, discussed with the employee, and documented in the employee's annual performance appraisal record." In this way, midlevel administrators and above are clear on expectations and their ownership of assessment as a vital responsibility.

Another forum in which this can occur is new employee onboarding. During the onboarding process, communication with new employees whose position responsibilities include assessment must be clear about how their work is vital to achieving goals and how they will be held accountable. Similar to annual ethics training, during which employees are required to complete an online course and affirm that they have read and understood the content, staff should be required to sign an assessment-related competencies document.

Tell the Story Through Knowing the Data

Those who work in student affairs assessment recognize the importance of assessment and data ownership. It is imperative to accept responsibilities for actions, including knowing the types and methods of assessments, understanding how results are used to accurately reflect what is working and what is not, accepting responsibility for mistakes, and acknowledging all limitations. As numbers can be just as ambiguous as words, student affairs professionals who conduct assessment, including the SSAO, also experience ownership by demonstrating their ability to interpret and speak accurately about assessment results. Owning the data signifies capacity and commitment to conducting rigorous statistical analyses without manipulation and/or misrepresentation of the data in order to produce a desired outcome. In the words of Mark Twain, "There are lies, damned lies, and statistics." The preservation of trust and integrity through assessment and data ownership cannot be compromised. When staff feel ownership, they are more likely to want to make what they own better, perhaps even wanting to own even more.

Provide Annual Assessment Presentations

Another approach for engaging staff in a commitment to assessment is for the SSAO of student affairs to routinize annual assessment presentations. Each unit director, for example, would be charged with providing a concise presentation to the division or designated audience describing what they perceive to be the most important assessment during the past year. They would describe the assessment goal, the measurable outcome(s), the evaluation strategy, the method(s) used to disseminate the findings, and, most importantly, what actions were taken as a direct result of the findings. Directors might describe how a program or service was improved, where the results on student learning or development were shown, what change in policy or procedure was instituted, or why a program or service was discontinued. If no change occurred, directors would provide evidence justifying continuing current practice. Formalizing and sharing assessment data would serve to reinforce ownership and create opportunities for collaboration and information among colleagues. All in all, assessment and data ownership are critical to the continued advancement of student affairs.

Give Rewards and Feedback

The SSAO and the leadership team who consistently reward good assessment practice and fairly impose consequences associated with failing to demonstrate evidence of assessment have the ability to positively affect sustainability. Critically, though, these actions must be communicated to the entire division. Assessment that provides evidence of measurably effective programs and services is obviously validating and confidence boosting. Results from assessment indicating that a program or service is weak and ineffective, however, provide us with the opportunity to act on assessment's principal value and make improvements and demonstrate evidence-based decision making.

Systematic assessment is defined as the ongoing process of collecting, interpreting, and acting on data and information. Assessment practices become commonplace over time and are administered at common points across the year. From a systems perspective, staff are intertwined with ownership of assessment and are expected to set clear goals, regularly measure those goals, periodically report evidence of success, and continuously work to improve results. Findings from the process are visited on a repeated basis in order to ensure that progress toward goals is made.

Sustainability requires dedicated leadership that is fully and visibly engaged, uses a common language (as discussed in Chapter 7), establishes standardized processes and procedures that are both followed and enforced, creates an infrastructure to support assessment efforts, and follows a practice of recognizing and celebrating successes. Systemic and systematic assessment aligned with the institution's and division's mission, values, and goals positively impacts our capacity to create and sustain buy-in.

Engage in Creative Infusion

As has been discussed, some staff perception of assessment is less than enthusiastic; we are especially challenged to engage these colleagues in their commitment to assessment. Assessment practitioners are encouraged to innovatively infuse assessment into staff meetings, workshops, and so on. Regarding assessment, thinking outside the box is more than just a business cliché; it's taking an approach that is new and unique.

One example of creatively infusing assessment was recently used at the beginning of an assessment workshop at the Georgia Institute of Technology. Twelve staff members in attendance each had a "clicker," a response system intended to promote engagement and active learning. Figure 4.1, taken from *Building a Culture of Evidence in Student Affairs* (Culp & Dungy, 2012, p. 13), has a table of 10 assessment terms and definitions. A slide of the table

Table 4.1 Assessment Terminology

Assessment Term	Definition
1. Culture of evidence	A. "Any effort to gather, analyze, and interpret evidence that describes institutional, departmental, divisional, or agency effectiveness" (Upcraft & Schuh, 1996, p. 18)
2. Curriculum mapping	B. "Any effort to use assessment evidence to improve institutional, departmental, or agency effectiveness" (Upcraft & Schuh, 1996, p. 19)
3. Traditional assessment	C. Use of multiple choice, true or false, fill-in-the-blanks, and similar assessments to determine whether students have learned what they were supposed to learn
4. Authentic assessment	D. Measures learning by asking students to apply the knowledge they have acquired to real-world tasks
5. Assessment	E. Scoring strategy to measure learning outcomes that lists the criteria used to determine the extent to which students have mastered the tasks, skills, or knowledge associated with a program, service, activity, or class
6. Developmental outcome	F. Determines whether and to what degree students have learned what they were supposed to have learned by participating in a student affairs–sponsored program, service, activity, experience, or class
7. Program outcome	G. Determines whether student affairs programs, services, activities, experiences, or classes accomplish what they are designed to accomplish
8. Learning outcome	H. Determines whether and to what degree student behaviors, beliefs, or values change as a result of participation in a student affairs–sponsored program, service, activity, or class
9. Rubric	I. A commitment among student affairs professionals to demonstrate, using hard data, how the programs they offer, the processes they implement, and the services they provide are effective and contribute in a significant way to the institution's ability to reach its stated goals and fulfill its mission
10. Evaluation	J. A process designed to show a clear relationship between the institution's general education outcomes or key performance indicators and specific courses, programs, services, or activities

Note: From Culp & Dungy, 2012, p. 33. Reprinted with permission.

was displayed and participants were asked to match each assessment term with the best-fitting definition. Participant responses for each definition varied greatly, with few respondents correctly matching the term with its definition. Close to the workshop end, the exercise was repeated with a significantly higher number of correct responses. The clickers provided a mechanism for staff to participate anonymously and integrated a "game approach" that clearly engaged them.

Build Trust and Relationships

Although it may seem obvious, creating and sustaining assessment buy-in unquestionably requires building and nurturing relationships with others. It is the responsibility of those who are tasked with championing assessment (whether the coordinator, the chair of the assessment team, or the SSAO) to meet regularly with division staff. As those responsible for assessment listen and learn, they will develop an understanding of staff assessment competencies, identify fears and barriers, and conceptualize shared strategies for making assessment workable for staff. As a result, they will generate assessment allies, help staff see why assessment matters, and lay the foundation for a more sustained buy-in. Ultimately they will develop trust among staff and create positive working relationships. There are two primary strategies for building and maintaining relationships: (a) schedule frequent and meaningful interactions and (b) provide timely and responsive feedback and help.

Intentional, meaningful, and frequent interaction communicates the division's continued commitment to assessment and affirms that the collection, analysis, use, and reporting of assessment results can and does provide evidence of the value of divisional programs and services. Assessment discussions ought to be conducted in the unit's work space. Meeting colleagues in their work environment conveys a degree of respect and allows others to "see" assessment staff, which is particularly important for those who play games of avoidance, especially around deadlines for assessment plans and reports. It allows for safe and candid discussions and increases the likelihood that consistent messages and accurate information will be relayed and received. Such meetings should be scheduled on a regular basis as well as organized ad hoc. For example, a minimum of two scheduled meetings a semester may be needed to create the foundation, but additional meetings may be required to progress toward increased understanding and competence.

Frequent interaction must extend beyond face time and can occur via e-mail or other communications. It is important to provide useful assessment-related information to division colleagues on a regular basis. In addition to uploading reports and resources on the student affairs website, assessment staff need to be intentional about sending colleagues assessment materials, including new research publications and other contributions to the body of assessment in student affairs literature or announcements regarding webinars and structured conversations, as well as local and national assessment conferences. Such resources may be provided by Student Affairs Assessment Leaders (SAAL), an organization that has offered student affairs assessment practitioners expert advice, current research and publications, and ally support. SAAL's main goal is to furnish student affairs assessment practitioners with opportunities to collaborate and discuss issues for the purpose of improving assessment efforts in student affairs. SAAL members have varying degrees of knowledge and assessment expertise but are exceptionally welcoming to newcomers and responsive to questions posed on the listserv (studentaffairsassessment.org).

As those who coordinate assessment increase time spent with and resources provided to staff, decades of educational research also support the notion that *less* teaching and *more* feedback results in greater learning (Bransford, Brown, & Cocking, 2000; Hattie, 2008; Marzano, Pickering, & Pollock, 2001). In our efforts to build assessment capacity, timely feedback to questions and requests for assistance will improve our ability to establish and maintain assessment buy-in. Regardless of the number of staff in the division's office of assessment, timeliness of response is crucial to the assessment process. When staff encounter challenges associated with an assessment project, it serves both the division and institution well to provide assistance as soon as feasible, because, as noted in previous chapters, staff often do not feel competent with assessment procedures. Failing to respond to calls for assistance negatively impacts trust and increases the likelihood of producing unreliable results, which may ultimately jeopardize the integrity of the assessment project. Timely feedback can mitigate or prevent such unfortunate results.

At each step in the assessment process, information gleaned can be used to inform the next or previous step. Providing timely, documented responses to staff members who raise questions or work on the project builds assessment skill capacity, consistently conveys the message that assessment is valued and supported, and fosters relationships. Engaging in open, forthright discussions, regardless of the assessment results, develops relationships, builds trust, and has the potential to boost confidence. The documentation and discussion of assessment projects is essential to increasing staff assessment competencies, communicating what was learned, and using the results for data-based decision making.

Consider the Ethical Implications of Assessment

In discussing strategies intended to engage staff with respect to their commitment to assessment, we would be remiss to omit the ethical implications. As student affairs professionals, we all have ethical obligations such as integrity, honesty, confidentiality, professional competency, public safety, and fairness. When ethical standards are not followed, numerous negative outcomes can occur, including less valuable results if there are suspicions that the data are contaminated by bias or special interests, thus risking the credibility and effectiveness of the division and the institution.

Among the challenges associated with ensuring ethical assessment practice is a situational dilemma referred to in psychology as a *multiple relationship*. Often, staff members performing the assessment at an institution are involved with various institutional activities, as either participants or organizers. The dilemma arises when the staff need to provide an assessment on the effectiveness of the program in which they are participating, as the individual who is doing the assessment may be directly affected by the report he or she gives; this situation could easily compromise the credibility of the assessment itself. This ethical error can be avoided by ensuring that the assessment project leader/team neither has ownership of nor would be directly impacted by the results. Using persons outside of the department, such as an assessment coordinator, to conduct such assessments may help minimize ethical risks.

Another ethical rule that applies to not only student affairs assessment, but assessment in general, is confidentiality. One of the first rules of data collection in assessment is the protection of the confidentiality of one's sources, including safe storage of confidential records. If confidentiality is not protected, negative assessments could result in a degree of retaliation upon the sources. If participants know that the information they provide can be traced back to them, they are less likely to disclose any underlying issues that may be occurring. One strategy for preventing this ethical error is by safeguarding storage. Research participants should be advised that the data collected about them will be kept private to the extent allowed by law. Staff can protect privacy by storing information by code rather than by name. Staff must ensure that records will be kept in locked files, only study staff will be allowed to examine them, and no identifiers will be included when results of the study are presented or published.

The Department of Student Life Studies at Texas A&M University has among the most robust standards of ethical practice (studentlifestudies .tamu.edu/about/standards). The standards have been adapted from the Association for Institutional Research's Code of Ethics, CAS Characteristics of Individual Excellence for Professional Practice in Higher Education, and the CAS Statement of Shared Ethical Principles. The standards reflect the institution's commitment to promoting high ethical standards for staff behavior as they work with assessments and speak to competence, practice, and confidentiality.

Our ability to conduct research using human subjects is a privilege granted to us by society for the advancement of knowledge and the improvement of the human condition. Student affairs assessment would be significantly advanced if all institutions developed, prominently published, and consistently practiced high ethical standards.

Conclusion

Creating and sustaining buy-in to assessment within divisions of student affairs is a fundamental and continuous aspect of any assessment program. Student affairs assessment practitioners must be relentless in their efforts to obtain the acceptance of and commitment to the practice of comprehensive assessment. By achieving and maintaining assessment buy-in, student affairs organizations have a greater likelihood of influencing institutional policy and practice, securing fiscal and human resources, and demonstrating the value of their programs and services.

This chapter builds on previous chapter discussions, in that it further explains why assessment matters and how SSAOs can begin to create the staff buy-in that is so important when trying to develop a positive culture of assessment. We address how an SSAO might specifically counter staff arguments, as well as ways to build assessment culture. The next chapter focuses on ways to recognize and reward staff who become aligned with divisional assessment culture.

References

Baker, G. R., Jankowski, N. A., Provezis, S., & Kinzie, J. (2012). *Using assessment results: Promising practices of institutions that do it well.* Urbana, IL: University of Illinois–Indiana University & National Institute for Learning Outcomes Assessment (NILOA).

Bransford, J. D., Brown, A. L., & Cocking, R. R. (Eds.). (2000). *How people learn: Brain, mind, experience, and school.* Washington, DC: National Academy Press.

Culp, M. M. & Dungy, G. J. (2012). *Building a culture of evidence in student affairs: A guide for leaders and practitioners.* Washington, DC: NASPA.

Hattie, J. (2008). *Visible learning: A synthesis of over 800 meta-analyses relating to achievement.* New York, NY: Routledge.

Marzano, R., Pickering, D., & Pollock, J. (2001). *Classroom instruction that works: Research-based strategies for increasing student achievement.* Alexandria, VA: Association for Supervision and Curriculum Development.

Upcraft, M. L., & Schuh, J. H. (1996). *Assessment in student affairs: A guide for practitioners.* San Francisco, CA: Jossey-Bass.

5

TENET FIVE: IMPLEMENT ACCOUNTABILITY AND SUPPORT STRUCTURES TO ENCOURAGE ASSESSMENT

Emily Burris Hester and Kurt J. Keppler

SSAO's Perspective

Kurt J. Keppler

Institutional leadership must embrace and champion assessment to change the way assessment is viewed by a department or division. If those at the top level of each organizational structure view assessment simply as a requirement to be checked off a list, then professionals in those areas will find it difficult to utilize assessment in an impactful way. Within student affairs, commitment begins with the senior student affairs officer (SSAO) and must trickle down to each supervisory level. Senior leadership must create clear expectations in addition to communicating the vision and providing necessary resources for departments to conduct assessment. Departmental leadership must then take that combination of expectations, visions, and resources to create the action plan for ensuring that quality assessment happens within their department. Each level of the structure has a vital role in the process and all must be accountable to not only the supervisors but also the assessment professional (Keeling, Wall, Underhile, & Dungy, 2008).

With assessment as a key expectation of all professional staff, the SSAO must establish systems and infrastructure to achieve maximum performance. In previous chapters, authors have focused on the overall infrastructure needed; once the SSAO attends to culture and has achieved some level of buy-in from all staff, there must be ways in which assessment practices become an expectation. Ultimately, when assessment is needed, its success depends on the degree to which staff are able and willing to meet expectations. Although staff concerns about competence and confidence must be addressed, there comes a time when all who are involved in administering student affairs work should be simply expected to perform vital responsibilities such as assessing their programs and services. It is, however, imperative that the SSAO provide the support necessary to help motivate staff to engage in assessment so they can improve the programs and services offered by the division.

    The practice of meeting expectations often stems from two strategies: holding people accountable and providing incentives and recognition. This chapter explains why such approaches matter as SSAOs and divisional leaders seek to make assessment an ongoing part of student affairs work using the notion of challenge and support as a framework.

Previous chapters discuss steps to create a culture of assessment and outline sound practices to bring those concepts to life. It is imperative that the SSAO is involved in not only holding staff accountable for assessment but also motivating them through unique incentives. Throughout this chapter we will get back to the basics with a new twist on the theory of challenge and support while building on the concepts and practices discussed in earlier chapters. Sanford's (1966) theory of challenge and support proposes that students grow best when adequate and appropriate amounts of challenge and support are provided. In an environment in which too much challenge is demanded without adequate support, the result is increased anxiety and defensiveness among individuals. If the opposite occurs and too much support is provided, then ownership does not occur and unresponsiveness tends to be the main outcome. Challenge and support must be in balance to achieve the desired educational outcomes. These same concepts that have been applied to college students using Sanford's theory can easily be translated to professional staff, specifically as it relates to their work in assessment. Finding the balance between challenging staff members and supporting their work as they grow and practice assessment can help make assessment a positive experience in both the outcomes and experience of the staff involved.

Challenge

The term *challenge* often indicates a roadblock or issue we are facing. However, in our current practice, it is important to move away from the notion of challenge as a barrier and focus on it as a way to open opportunities for staff development and motivation. In the pages that follow, we discuss how to use motivation and accountability to engage staff in a culture of assessment.

We often focus on what we "can't do" or things we "don't have." In Chapter 3, the authors shared common excuses for why professionals don't, won't, or can't engage in assessment. The responses to those excuses provided a reframe by using motivation and accountability to focus on what we "can do" and skills we "do have" in the area of assessment. As assessment leaders, we should challenge notions and present new ways of doing assessment so that staff see it as a challenge to grow. When the balance is struck between challenge and support, it is the challenge that propels the individual forward toward maximum growth.

Motivation as a Vehicle for Challenge

When we think of motivation as a vehicle to help challenge our staff, we open a new approach to how we talk to staff about assessment. Staff are motivated in different ways. Some are motivated by public recognition, whereas others may be motivated by a reward for completing what is often seen as an add-on to their current work. To challenge our professionals in their assessment practice, we must do more than merely lay out expectations or issue a verbal command. Challenge requires positive motivation and an understanding of what drives your staff members. It is important to consider a variety of ways to satisfy individuals depending on what motivates them, with two examples being rewards and recognition.

Motivation Through Rewards

1. *Create an innovation fund.* Show staff that assessment is truly valued through setting aside funds to reward good assessment or positive changes to a program using assessment results. When staff can see that funds are available to support their work, then the challenge isn't empty chatter. Staff may be reenergized to give assessment their full effort and realize that innovating is important to their work.

2. *Reward outstanding individuals.* Consider staff who show outstanding commitment and excellence in assessment for special raises, merit pools to give additional small percentage raises, or promotions to show the significance of assessment. This helps validate that individual work and excellence in assessment is a highly valued skill within your division.

3. *Encourage conference presentations.* Fund staff travel to professional conferences if they are using evidence to inform the field of new practices or ways to conduct assessment. This sets a clear expectation that assessment

is a foundation of student affairs work, allows the staff member to contribute to the field, brings recognition for your university's student affairs division, and gives staff the opportunity to attend conferences that may be seen as a valued "perk."

Motivation Through Recognition

1. *Distribute divisional assessment awards.* At annual divisional gatherings in which awards are presented, use the opportunity to highlight best practices within your division. For example, each year Portland State University gives out two assessment awards—one titled "Excellence and Innovation in Assessment" and another called "Emerging Best Practice in Assessment."
2. *Celebrate creativity.* Recognize assessment projects that have used methods other than a standard survey of staff professionals and employed a variety of tools such as focus groups, phone polling, blog reports, social media, and so on.
3. *Nominate staff or programs for professional association awards and/or leadership positions.* Don't limit the award recognition to your campus—think big and nominate staff or programs that are evidence-based for professional association awards. You may also encourage or nominate outstanding assessment professionals to apply for leadership positions in professional associations.
4. *Apply for grants.* Often when we think of grant funding, we think of a long and difficult process; however, look to professional associations and other organizations for opportunities for grants. Typically, assessment is a major component of the application process, a win-win as it provides both recognition and funding for a project. For example, the National Association of Student Personnel Administrators (NASPA) offers an Assessment, Evaluation, and Research Knowledge Community Assessment and Research Grant each year, awarding an institution up to $1,000.

Institutional Examples of Rewards and Recognition

At Weber State University, a hybrid of public recognition and reward is used to highlight great assessment within the Division of Student Affairs. Each year, student affairs assessment puts out an assessment progress report for each department evaluated on a rubric using a 1–4 scale. Departments are evaluated in areas including student headcounts, needs and satisfaction, cohort data, student learning outcomes, and strategic plans. Those departments that score 3.5 or above are eligible for the divisional assessment award. Then a subcommittee of the assessment committee reviews the finalists and discusses their progress reports, their improvement over time, and any innovative assessment practices that their department may have used to select a winner. The winner is then "blessed" by the Student Affairs Management Council. The winner is recognized publicly at the spring division meeting, and the department receives $500 to go toward assessment within their department.

In another example, at Virginia Tech, assessment is rewarded through an initiative that provides grants to departments within the division. According to the Office of Assessment and Evaluation newsletter:

> In 2010–2011, the first Closing the Loop Award was created to encourage faculty and staff in the division to create an assessment plan, carry out an assessment, and use the results to make recommendations for improvements based on the findings, i.e., "close the loop." The funds can be used to support the expansion and improvement of assessed programs and services in the Division of Student Affairs or implement recommendations based on assessment findings. Awards range from $500 to $2,500. The applications are reviewed annually by a panel of assessment experts from outside the division. (Glass, 2012, p. 3)

Accountability as a Vehicle for Challenge

The general theme of accountability is critical in accomplishing assessment goals (Upcraft & Schuh, 1996). For accountability, we revisit the concept of consistency in developing a culture of assessment. Consistency in messaging and regularity will keep the focus on assessment not only throughout the year, but also during planning cycles or peak assessment times. If assessment is regularly discussed in divisional or departmental meetings and discussions, it will more easily become a part of the culture within a unit rather than something done to satisfy a requirement. When it is part of the day-to-day language of staff, then no one can say "I forgot" and mean it with sincerity.

A key question that the SSAO should answer is: What happens when there is a lack of connection and outcomes are not achieved? Providing structure and guidance on how assessment results will be used within the divisional structure can help address fear or concerns. The SSAO and assessment leadership should express caring and concern for the assessment process within a department, although it is key that leadership doesn't excuse a lack of progress within a department. As addressed previously, time cannot be an excuse regardless of workload or administrative function; one must find ways to incorporate assessment within the student affairs structure.

Why Accountability Matters

As a case study, Jim has been the director of a department for eight years; prior to that he was an assistant director in the department for six years. He was hired in part because of his general likability. Furthermore, he advocates well for students and is invested in helping them plan and host successful programs. Although Jim works hard, there is little evidence about how his programs are contributing to desired goals in the division. He works with students to track attendance but rarely incorporates assessment, specifically of learning outcomes, into programs. The division has emphasized the collection of such evidence for the last four years.

As the SSAO you have informed Jim that he needs to provide more evidence of the influence of his programs, particularly during tight budget times. Jim often agrees but indicates that there are just not enough hours in the day. For two years he has heard your requests without much movement on assessment activities. Is it time to hold Jim accountable for his failure to prioritize assessment? Are there any rewards or recognition that might motivate Jim to engage in the assessment being requested? Are assessment results shared with peers at events like division-wide gatherings or staff meetings?

In this scenario, Jim has not been compliant with the requests of his SSAO to collect evidence of how programs are influencing the student experience. Considering that Jim has been asked previously and is, moreover, aware of the divisional push toward assessment, approaches to holding Jim accountable may be important. Considering next steps, it is important to understand why accountability matters generally and in the area of assessment in student affairs specifically.

In the scenario provided there are a lot of unanswered questions. Most important is why Jim is resistant to assessment. Does he feel inadequately trained to perform the task at hand? Is he concerned about the results he might find? Although he has noted that time is an issue, the truth is that Jim doesn't place value on assessment and has not made it a priority for himself or his staff. A key issue is that Jim has learned he can delay providing assessment data for more than two years. Accountability is a necessary part of challenge and support. If you are providing the support that is needed for staff to perform assessment, then the challenge is missing in this example. As described previously, when support is adequate but challenge is lacking, individuals stagnate—in Jim's case, for the past two years.

Accountability and rewards within each division should be made meaningful based on its unique organizational culture and context. SSAOs should keep a pulse on the ways in which rewards and recognition would be best received within their divisions. This could be done through utilizing focus groups of all levels of staff to learn overall perceptions of assessment recognition and dig into the rewards that would be most impactful. Alternatively, supervisors could identify meaningful recognition through the annual performance review processes when staff members may be setting professional development goals for the year.

Support

As mentioned previously, challenges are not adequate without support. But what does it mean to support staff as it relates to student affairs assessment? We have to think about support as more than simply a verbal "I support assessment," and ensure that staff have the tools they need to do assessment. According to Sanford (1966), when support is left out of the equation, then individuals who are only challenged retreat or shut down. Support is key for individuals to successfully develop assessment skills and increase the quality of their assessment work within the division.

One area that deserves a serious look is how to support assessment within the current budget. In other words, is assessment supported in divisional professional development initiatives? Often we rely on what is free and/or easy to do when it comes to professional development in assessment or expect staff to take advantage of no-cost opportunities on their own. Instead, we should make professional development in assessment an intentional focus that is ongoing.

The key to support in this concept is ensuring that staff have the tools to do good assessment. In this case, the tools are knowledge and training as well as technology, time, and supervisory support. Using a model for creating an "assessment army" of educated professionals within your division is one that typically takes time but ultimately provides benefit for both the individual and the division. For example, the University of Georgia's Department of Student Affairs Assessment uses a cohort model for practitioners from various departments to form an "A-team," which equips team members with the assessment basics. A new A-team is selected each year, and their meetings provide both professional training and a support system for staff members.

Utilizing this team training model is only one way to help train staff in the area of assessment; each division must find the model that works best for them. Many universities use division-wide professional development to train staff utilizing webinars and/or staff presentations. For example, at Louisiana State University, to show the value of assessment, the divisional professional development committee has indicated strong support by including nationally renowned assessment speakers as a part of the division-wide investment in capacity building and opportunities for conversations focused around assessment. This yearly focus allows assessment to be an active and evident value for the entire division.

You may also reframe the conversation based on professional competencies. The joint publication *ACPA/NASPA Professional Competency Areas for Student Affairs Practitioners* (American College Personnel Association & National Association of Student Personnel Administrators, 2010) includes the primary competency "Assessment, Evaluation, and Research." According to the publication,

> The Assessment, Evaluation, and Research competency area (AER) focuses on the ability to use, design, conduct, and critique qualitative and quantitative AER analyses; to manage organizations using AER processes and the results obtained from them; and to shape the political and ethical climate surrounding AER processes and uses on campus. (p. 8)

If we reframe assessment as a competency in the field, it becomes important to our professional success and allows support to be structured in training, creating space for the learning of these skills. This also will bring forth a culture of assessment where assessment is just part of what we do rather than being viewed as an add-on, which then continues to build and help the division make leaps forward in assessment competency building in individual staff members.

Another form of support is creating the space to learn and fail together as staff learn how to assess appropriately. Whereas tackling an assessment project may seem daunting for an individual new to assessment (or one falsely perceived as seasoned), the practice of assessment may be better learned through group assessment projects. Divide staff into teams to provide the "group project" learning environment that we know works in the classroom for students. Encourage the groups to brainstorm, discuss, and hash out the best way to take an assessment project from its infancy to completion. Provide feedback to the group at each step along the way in the same manner that a faculty member might provide feedback on a student's rough draft or outline. This helps staff know they are going in the right direction but allows them to learn through doing. This circles back to the discussion in Chapter 3 of embracing the role of educator, but in this case involves also embracing the role of learner.

Similar learning groups could be set up through utilizing assessment committees or learning partnerships. As mentioned in Chapter 3 about building an assessment culture, support is not just about staff getting the job done but creating a safe space to learn and apply new skills related to assessment. You may also think of assessment training as an apprenticeship, assigning staff a coach or mentor who is an experienced professional with strong assessment skills. Using a coaching model allows the mentor to teach staff about assessment and provide feedback as they engage in the actual work of assessment. Often staff members feel that if their assessment practice fails or is subpar then it means *they* have failed as professionals. The coach or mentor can have those conversations about what happens when we don't get the outcomes desired in a safe learning space.

Conclusion

Throughout this chapter we have provided recommendations and examples of the ways in which to balance challenge and support for staff as it relates to assessment within student affairs. Evaluating the current model for accountability and ways in which staff are rewarded and recognized within your division is a first step toward creating and sustaining assessment and providing the challenge and support that staff need in assessment work. Always keep in mind the importance of the balance between challenge and appropriate support by confirming that staff have the tools, especially training and space to learn, to properly engage both as individuals and as a department in assessment.

Within this section of the book, the focus is on establishing the expectations for and strengthening the culture of assessment. Garrison Duncan and Holmes address ways to counter assessment arguments. Woods and Schafer provide strategies to infuse assessment into the culture of a division of student affairs. In this chapter, Hester and Keppler focus on specific ways to provide challenge and support for staff. In the next chapter, Adams-Gaston and Kennedy-Phillips revisit the four Cs that Garrison Duncan and Holmes identify as key strategies to addressing assessment concerns and explain how these four Cs are also vital to anchoring assessment into the long-term culture of a division of student affairs.

References

American College Personnel Association & National Association of Student Personnel Administrators. (2010). *ACPA/NASPA professional competency areas for student affairs practitioners.* Washington, DC: Author.

Glass, M. (2012, Spring). Creating a culture of assessment in the division of student affairs. *Assessment in Action,* 2–3.

Keeling, R. P., Wall, A. F., Underhile, R., & Dungy, G. J. (2008). *Assessment reconsidered.* Washington, DC: NASPA.

Sanford, N. (1966). *Self and society: Social change and individual development.* New York, NY: Atherton.

Upcraft, M. L., & Schuh, J. (1996) *Assessment in student affairs: A guide for practitioners.* San Francisco, CA: Jossey-Bass.

6

TENET SIX: ANCHOR CULTURAL CHANGE

Javaune Adams-Gaston and Lance C. Kennedy-Phillips

SSAO's Perspective

Javaune Adams-Gaston

Colleagues from across the nation regularly contact me to inquire about our assessment team at the Center for the Study of Student Life. Many are surprised to learn that we have assembled a group of PhD researchers, supporting analysts, and several upper-division student employees. This talented group is dedicated to studying, researching, and assessing the learning and development of college students, at Ohio State and across the nation, while also directing and coordinating the research and assessment needs of the Office of Student Life's more than 40 departments.

The first question many colleagues ask is: How are you able to dedicate that level of resources to assessment? I usually answer with a question of my own: How can I afford not to?

All student affairs divisions should develop a culture of evidence to support the decision-making processes of the division and the university. But to develop and sustain a culture of evidence in student affairs one must have commitment, consistency, connection, and communication, which have been previously identified in this book by Garrison Duncan and Holmes as vital to creating culture. Sustaining a culture of evidence and assessment is not easy and it is not accomplished overnight. This chapter explains the four components necessary for student affairs organizations to sustain a culture of evidence.

Over months and years, I have worked with my executive team and unit directors on these components to establish expectations and a supportive structure while empowering my assessment team to lead our organizational effort. Accordingly, it has been important to provide the tools for our staff members to be successful (easy-to-use annual reporting systems, systematic strategic planning processes, generalized and specific training opportunities, annual assessment conferences, etc.). One of the single most important things I have been able to do to support a culture of assessment is to "close the loop" with the data they are providing to me. I regularly feature their results and model the importance of sharing: in presentations and speeches, with my weekly column to students and parents, and through meetings and informal conversations. I also make a point to ensure that presentations to our university's senior leaders, particularly those to the board of trustees, are data rich and evidence driven.

Although the 24/7 nature of our work may sometimes require us to make on-the-spot decisions for the welfare of our students, "going with our gut" is not sustainable when developing long-term strategic plans for the future. Likewise, it is wonderful and necessary to be able to share touching individual student stories about growth and success, but equally important is our ability to back up these stories with quantifiable results about how our work has been sustainably successful for many students. We live in a "return on investment" world, and without a strong foundation of assessment, we would simply be unable to answer the crucial questions when seeking approval for an important student service or when demonstrating how our efforts contribute to overall student success and the institution's academic mission.

The Four Components of Sustained Assessment Culture in Student Affairs

Some scholars define *culture* as the beliefs, values, or assumptions shared by all members of an organization (Schein, 1992). Studies that take this approach, which Joanne Martin (1992) calls the "integration perspective" (p. 45), tend to assume that values are clear and are "shared by all members of a culture, in an organization-wide consensus" (p. 45) and that members clearly understand their roles in the culture. Studies organized around the integration perspective often have the express goal of utilizing culture to manage behavior and beliefs and only acknowledge the existence of conflict and subcultures at a surface level. With this in mind, a student affairs organization must develop shared values, beliefs, and assumptions to be effective. The foundation of any student affairs culture has integrated into itself a system of operations, values, beliefs, and assumptions that are collectively authored and commonly accepted. Within student affairs and student affairs assessment culture, we believe that commitment, consistency, connection, and communication are components specifically valued.

Commitment

For any culture of evidence to be sustained and successful, it needs not only executive support but also ownership from all levels of the division. The culture will not be successful without a charge from the senior student affairs officer (SSAO), who sets the tone for the division. If the SSAO provides only casual support for assessment and data collection, the effectiveness of these actions diminishes immediately. The executive charge legitimizes the process, crucial when you are attempting to devise and establish a culture that cascades to all levels of the division. This must be intentional or the division runs the risk of becoming superfluous and your services won't fit the needs of students.

In addition to the SSAO, a senior-level professional must lead the assessment and data collection for the division. According to Kotter and Cohen (2002) "[assessment] initiatives flounder because they're headed up by people who lack the time or the clout to accomplish what is necessary" (p. 87). The leader of the process should report to the SSAO. The assessment and data professional must be able to provide insight into the division's mission and strategy. A strong sponsor can help push the process as it hits the inevitable stalls along the way. In other words, this person must be committed to the development of the culture of evidence and be able to intercede when the process encounters barriers.

Another aspect of *commitment* comes in the form of resources. The clearest way to show commitment to creating a culture of evidence is by providing the financial and staffing resources necessary to maintain and build the culture. For example, there should at least be one full-time professional designated to lead the assessment function. That professional should be supported by staff members specifically tasked to do the work if the institution size is sufficiently large, or at least be able to rely on designated staff members across the division who can conduct assessment and research.

Building staff capacity to do assessment is another element of sustaining a strong culture of evidence. Fear and lack of confidence are common reasons that assessment processes fail. We advocate sending staff members to professional institutes about assessment and data collection sponsored in many areas of the country. Both the National Association of Student Personnel Administrators (NASPA) and the American College Personnel Association (ACPA) sponsor conferences and webinar series that are specifically targeted toward building assessment capacity.

Consistency

With the cyclical nature of our student body and entry-level to midlevel staff, *consistency* is the most difficult component to achieve. Assessment and evidence gathering must become part of the institutional process. Just as we develop budgets and content for our programs and services, we must also develop clear outcomes and methods for assessing those outcomes. Building a culture is more than just designating "the year of assessment." The assessment process should not change every year. The process should be grounded in best practices and fit the unique needs of the organization. The greatest barrier to staff members committing to a culture of evidence is changing the process for collecting evidence every two to three years. By remaining consistent, the organization will be able to collect reliable longitudinal data, and staff members will see how these data support their work. The Ohio State University Office of Student Life has invested in the development of a reporting system (cssl.osu.edu/student-life-reporting) that automates the evidence collection process for the division. The system stores data chronologically so that patterns can be analyzed and decisions made based on trends in the data. The department head, in consultation with the supervising associate vice president, defines what data are collected. The office of the vice president for student life manages the overall process, and all data collected through this process belong to the division. These data contribute to telling the larger narrative of the division and its impact on student success and learning.

Consistency also means clarity of what constitutes good assessment. An outcomes-driven organization should have its practices and activities grounded in *measurable*, *manageable*, and *meaningful* expected outcomes, or the "3 Ms of Assessment." *Measurable* assessment is easy to categorize. When you ask a research or assessment question, is it measurable? Can you think of a quantitative or qualitative way to provide evidence that you are reaching that goal? *Manageable* assessment is incredibly important; assessments should be streamlined and part of our everyday work. You are likely to gather more general data to show that you are on target to achieve your goals. In addition, rather than trying to examine all aspects of your work in detail, focus on one in-depth assessment project at a time. Over a few years, you should be able to look at all of your outcomes in detail. Finally, assessment needs to be *meaningful,* a goal that can be difficult to achieve. Producing surveys or focus groups just to answer a question is not enough. Actually utilizing the results instead of letting those results sit on a shelf is imperative. Be aware, however, that this portion takes time to achieve.

A consistent and reliable assessment and evidence-collection process can yield strong trend data for the organization and having strong trend data can bolster a culture of evidence. When an organization's staff members have reliable data, they can make positive data-informed change. They can see growth over time and make adjustments to programs and services when necessary. Good trend data means that decisions can be based on solid information rather than inferences based on one or two, possibly outlier, academic terms.

Connection

A strong and sustained culture of evidence is *connected* to the larger university mission and goals. Student affairs divisions must be able to demonstrate that their work aligns with university values so that senior staff can secure monetary and personnel resources, participate in institutional accreditation, and help students develop the skills necessary to achieve career success. Student affairs divisions contribute to all of these aspects of the university; by aligning and mapping a division's data and evidence with those of the larger institution, the story, or evidence, is clear, strong, and persuasive.

Connection is also important for increasing staff motivation and momentum to assess programming and services and to gather data. Staff members want to know that their work is connected to the larger university narrative; assessment does not take place in a vacuum. The Ohio State University takes a "One University" approach to assessment. Staff members from many areas of the university participate in communities of practice around various issues and interests such as diversity, wellness, enrollment, and global citizenship. A community of practice brings diverse perspectives together to address a commonly agreed-upon issue or question. Showing staff members how their work *connects* to the achievement of university outcomes may help to link the various touch points that lead to student learning and success. Demonstrating these connections to staff members may make them more interested in collaborating across the institution in the hope that these collaborations will lead to increased student learning and success.

Another aspect of connection is the realization that learning takes place at all levels of the organization. An integrated assessment process will help make clear the connections among various levels of outcomes while also mapping and aligning outcomes back to the larger divisional goals. For example, the Office of Student Life at The Ohio State University, through good assessment, was able to provide evidence for how its social justice engagement program was supporting the university's goal of increased global citizenship. According to Pelletier, Oaks, and Kennedy-Phillips (2013), "The most specific will be the program- or activity-level outcomes, and the broadest/most general will be the division-level outcomes" (p. 22). As Maki (2004) stated, "There is an underlying coherence [among levels of outcomes] that contributes to student learning" (p. 62). Without a connected assessment and evidence-collection process, it is difficult to understand and almost impossible to demonstrate where learning is taking place and how the division is connected to students' learning processes. Often the true point of evidence takes place at the program or activity level.

Communication

Without transparent, clear, and frequent *communication,* it is impossible to develop or implement a sustained and strong culture of evidence. Communication regarding the division's assessment process should involve all layers of the organization. Failure to clearly articulate the assessment process may lead to confusion and frustration. The language describing the process should be clear. Divisions should develop a glossary of terms. This helps prevent unnecessary barriers regarding participation in the process. Having consistency in language is key to any culture and is especially necessary for a culture built around evidence.

Strong cultures communicate results effectively. It is important to communicate results of assessments and research regularly to all members of the community. Sharing evidence with senior administrators and board members puts the division in charge of narratives around key issues regarding cocurricular experiences. Proactively sharing data with faculty members sends the message that student affairs is an active participant and contributor to student learning. Finally, sharing assessment results with students demonstrates that their voices are being heard. By communicating data in this way, the division establishes a reputation for providing regular and reliable reports and lays the foundation and establishes expectations for receiving evidence in this form from the division.

A key responsibility of communication when establishing a culture of evidence is to celebrate best practices within the division. For example, at Ohio State we collect card-swipe data for various programs and services. The Office of Student Life has used swiped data in its counseling center to track how long a student had to wait before seeing a counselor. These data have provided meaningful information leading to the addition of new counselors due to extended wait times. Without thoughtful review of these data, they would have just been numbers taking up space in a database on someone's desktop. A strong and sustained culture of evidence encourages reflection and intentional change and then communicates the message that data have informed decisions.

Celebrating the positive work around assessment can provide staff members across the division the opportunity to demonstrate new ideas and techniques, while taking ownership of their assessment achievements. Communication about these practices shows that meaningful assessment is possible for staff members who may believe they don't have the skills or ideas to do a strong assessment. Celebration reinforces the commitment senior leaders have to creating and sustaining a strong culture of evidence.

Conclusion

No longer can divisions rely on anecdotal decision making. Decisions must be made based on data that are collected as part of a systematic and systemic process. Data provide a context to understand the effectiveness of programs and services offered by the division. Members of the division must receive training regarding how to collect student learning outcomes data both quantitatively and qualitatively, as well as through the use of mixed methods. These data enhance the discourse regarding what students are learning and add to the culture of evidence.

The problems facing most student affairs organizations are the result of an increase in the rate of change in the environment in which they operate and a failure to adapt to such changes. "Social and cultural trends, economic forces, population changes, new and emerging technologies, and issues of public policy will have powerful and lasting effects on the ability of colleges and universities to fulfill the demands of their mission and the expectations of their students and constituencies" (Keeling, 2004, p. 4). However, student affairs is full of examples of how culture can be created and sustained; assessment should be yet another example.

Creating a strong and sustained culture of evidence requires commitment, consistency, connection, and communication. The future of student affairs is centered on accountability, both internally and externally. Our constituents demand high-quality programs and services with clear measures of success and clearly reported outcomes. This is not possible if we do not create strong and sustained cultures of evidence. In summary, focus on the following to sustain student affairs assessment culture:

1. *Be committed.* For any culture of evidence to be sustained and successful, it needs *committed* executive support as well as ownership from all levels of the division.
2. *Be consistent.* Assessment and evidence gathering must become a *consistent* part of the routine institutional and divisional management process.
3. *Be connected.* A strong and sustained culture of evidence is *connected* to the larger university mission and goals.
4. *Be communicative.* Without transparent, clear, and frequent *communication,* it is impossible to develop a sustained and strong culture of evidence.

References

Keeling, R. (Ed.). (2004). *Learning reconsidered: A campus-wide focus on the student experience.* Washington, DC: National Association of Student Personnel Administrators & American College Personnel Association.

Kotter, J. P., & Cohen, D. S. (2002). *The heart of change: Real-life stories of how people change their organizations.* Boston, MA: Harvard Business School.

Maki, P. (2004). *Assessing for learning: Building a sustainable commitment across the institution.* Sterling, VA: Stylus.

Martin, J. (1992). *Cultures in organizations: Three perspectives.* Oxford: Oxford University Press.

Pelletier, J., Oaks, D. J., & Kennedy-Phillips, L. (2013). Grounded in reality: Writing learning outcomes. *The Bulletin, 81*(6). Retrieved from https://www.acui.org/publications/bulletin/article.aspx?issue=41800&id=23406

Schein, E. H. (1992). *Organizational culture and leadership.* San Francisco, CA: Jossey-Bass.

PART THREE

SOUND ASSESSMENT PRACTICES

"Practice does not make perfect. Perfect practice makes perfect."

—Vince Lombardi in *Run to Win: Vince Lombardi on Coaching and Leadership*
by Donald T. Phillips, 2001

There are many books that cover how to do assessment, from writing learning outcomes to designing a survey to writing an assessment report. However, what is missing from the literature is information about how senior student affairs officers can systemically set up the division in a way that encourages the use of sound assessment practices. Assessment can happen in many ways, but until it is focused on the division's goals, it is just practice. In the chapters that follow, best practices in assessment are identified and described with the senior student affairs officer in mind.

7

TENET SEVEN: DEVELOP ASSESSMENT PLANS

Darby Roberts

SSAO's Perspective

Kevin Jackson

What drew me to our profession is the notion that we can and do make a difference in students' lives. For 30 years now, I have been a part of this beautiful and sometimes chaotic process. I have experienced student affairs work at its best and, tragically, at its worst. My expectation is that in order to provide our best work on a consistent basis, we must have access to and utilize meaningful information. Our students deserve this, our institutions need this, and our society is increasingly demanding this. Put simply, in order to become better you must seek honest feedback and incorporate it into your ongoing planning and execution.

To do so requires that the leader explain why assessment is important as a means to an end (not the end itself) while reinforcing the need for collecting, sharing, and utilizing good information through more formal processes (division strategic plans, established goals and outcomes, budgeting, personnel decisions, etc.) as well as informal processes (division newsletters, kickoff luncheons, notes to staff, conversations with student leaders, etc.) and modeling the way through reflecting on and responding to ideas and issues based upon good information.

This past year, the division completed a division strategic plan and individual departmental operating plans that aligned with divisional strategic goals and outcomes. All of this work was completed within the broader context of a university vision process. Consequently, our planning process at the division level has been refined to be more mission centered, vision driven, and values based with an intentional set of goals, outcomes, and acts of determination framing how we approach our collective work. At the department level, each unit has established goals and outcomes and most have identified a set of action steps that are needed to accomplish them. In addition, each department has developed a general rubric for conducting an annual assessment. We are still working on the methodology for each assessment.

The division is entering our first annual budget cycle since completing the new division strategic plan and departmental operating plans. The first part of the budgeting process stipulates that departmental goals and outcomes be presented and emerging assessment data shared as the foundation upon which the department will discuss the effective use of existing resources and the need for additional resources. After each department presents its budget, our budget manager, deans, associate vice president, and I will meet to discuss compelling needs based on our strategic plan (which aligns with the university's vision document), departmental operational plans, and emerging assessment data. We will then identify or seek additional information about specific needs and ultimately decide whether to reallocate existing funds, recalibrate revenue/expenses and/or fund-raising goals to increase net income, and/or request new funds from the university centralized budgeting process in order to address a compelling need and/or move forward on a mission-centric opportunity. Having access to good assessment data is critical when working through the budget process. This need is amplified should we seek additional funds from the university, because we must not only have to prioritize the request from within our division but also effectively communicate the critical nature of the need or opportunity within a much broader environment of competing priorities.

Developing Assessment Plans

Senior student affairs officers (SSAOs) work in a complex, ever-changing environment and must answer to a variety of stakeholders to meet multiple demands. Within a division of student affairs, SSAOs and department heads are making decisions about budgeting, planning, and creating/elimating programs. To effectively do all of that, SSAOs must have consistent, usable information at their fingertips. Such information must be part of the infra-structure of a division of student affairs and processes should be systemic across departments. This chapter reviews the importance of developing assessment planning and reporting processes through an assessment cycle.

Within the institution or division, there should be a standard assessment cycle for each unit to follow. There are several models available, including those of Bresciani, Zelna, and Anderson (2004) and Suskie (2009). The Bresciani et al. cycle includes defining the mission/goals/outcomes around which the cycle flows, instituting program delivery methods, gathering and interpreting evidence, making decisions to improve programs and learning, planning for the future, and cultivating accountability. Suskie described the four-step assessment of the learning cycle as (a) establish learning goals, (b) provide learning opportunities, (c) assess student learning, and (d) use the results. Adopted cycles should not be overly complex but should resonate with the staff and provide a comprehensive structure to follow. The cycle should provide a systematic and continuous process. Clearly, the assessment cycle does not operate in a vacuum; external and institutional influences or changes may interrupt a smooth process. Budget cuts, the political environment, changes in institutional leadership, and new priorities can impact any given program at any given time. In addition, as research on students, student development, and learning outcomes is published, the information influences what we do and assess.

Assessment plans systematically describe a process in the future regarding data collection, interpretation, and use related to specific goals and outcomes. Although each institution can have a different model and timeline, there is some consistency in the process (see Appendix A for a sample template). The plans are usually submitted before the academic year begins to provide a road map with checkpoints. As an example, the Division of Student Affairs at Georgia Institute of Technology (Division of Student Affairs, 2014) has articulated its process on the division website. First, units identify approximately five operating and/or learning goals. Operational goals can address the division's customer service, impact on student development, programs, quality of service, and so on. The learning goals encompass what a student knows, feels, or is able to do. Second, units identify measurable outcomes for each goal. Third, units develop their evaluation strategy—how they will collect information to determine that an outcome has been achieved. This could include surveys, focus groups, observation, and so on. The plan should also include the timeline for data collection. Fourth, units identify how they will share and use the information for improvement. For example, sharing the information could include presentation at meetings or retreats. Following the data collection, units document the summary of results and the actions taken as a result of their assessment. The units not only describe the actual results, but also any interpretations and decisions (including continuing the current practice if appropriate). The actions could be a change in focus, budget, procedures, and so on.

At Northern Illinois University, the draft plans are due at the beginning of April for the department supervisor to give feedback and then to the student affairs assessment office in May for additional feedback. The final plans are due at the end of May. This gives the division leader an aggregate picture of assessment, particularly any opportunities for collaboration and identification of current issues. Their plans specifically include strategic priorities, relationship to core values, and academic collaboration, in addition to goals, outcomes, strategies, and data collection methods (Division of Student Affairs and Enrollment Management, 2014a).

Assessment reports provide information after the fact that includes results, conclusions, accomplishments, and actions. Without that structure, the SSAO is susceptible to receiving questionably valuable, random information at random times. Typically, assessment reports are due in early to midsummer to allow the SSAO to report to the president as needed before the end of the fiscal year (see Appendix B for a sample template). At Georgia Institute of Technology (Division of Student Affairs, 2014), each unit completes the established template and submits it to the SSAO. Some SSAOs combine the unit plans into a larger report about the accomplishments and future directions of the division (see saa.gatech.edu/uploads/files/2012 _2013FinalAssessmentReport.pdf).

At Northern Illinois University, the unit reports are incorporated into the Division of Student Affairs and Enrollment Management (2014b) *Annual Report,* which features exemplary programs/events and departmental priorities, mission, and highlights. The assessment reports provide information to the SSAO to make strategic decisions, but they can also be published in annual reports to share a valuable message with stakeholders.

Ideally, what divisions are assessing for improvement also aligns with the accountability expectations of external audiences (accreditation agencies, state agencies, etc.). Developing assessment plans and subsequent reports helps streamline reporting processes. In working through the assessment cycle, the external environment needs to be considered. The annual planning process should look at internal parameters (university, division, and unit vision, mission, goals, objectives, outcomes, and values). In addition, information should be provided about regional accreditation stipulations, state requirements, and system expectations (if the institution is part of a multi-institution system).

For example, Texas A&M University belongs to the Southern Association of Colleges and Schools Commission on Colleges (SACS) accreditation agency, which has clear requirements for assessing student learning in and out of the classroom and developing an institution-wide quality enhancement plan. In addition, Texas has created student learning outcomes, as has the Texas A&M University System. At the institution level, Texas A&M University has student learning outcomes for undergraduate, master's, and doctoral students. Although the three sets of learning outcomes overlap, they are not the same. The university also has instituted Vision 2020, a long-term strategic plan/direction and set of core values. The Division of Student Affairs has a vision, mission, guiding statements, goals, core values, and strategic plan. All of the departments in the division have a mission, goals, and outcomes illustrated in their assessment plans. Many also have their own vision, set of core values, and strategic plans. Larger departments may also have outcomes for specific units or programs. The whole process can become very frustrating at various reporting times if all of these components are not considered. On the other hand, it can become convoluted and cumbersome for staff to consider so many dimensions in their plans. In these cases, student affairs leaders can help shape the priorities into manageable tasks that support the core mission.

The Importance of Assessment Plans and Assessment Reports

Assessment plans and assessment reports are important to the existence of any unit. They are opportunities to illustrate alignment with and contributions to the larger organization's direction and priorities. In the current environment, student affairs needs to "tell our story" because not everyone knows how we contribute to student success, retention, and graduation. Some institutions have undergone restructuring that has eliminated divisions of student affairs. Although assessment documentation may not have changed those decisions in this politically charged environment, providing that information to high-level decision makers could provide evidence that a division is functioning well and working toward the institution's mission and priorities. Senior student affairs officers (or department heads) must consider whether they have the information at their fingertips that indicates value.

In particular, student learning outcomes assessment is key to providing evidence that student affairs does contribute to the overall education of students. Many institutions have outcomes related to degree programs/content knowledge, communication, working with others, diversity, critical thinking, and so on. Although a division may not be able to claim any contribution to knowledge of chemistry, engineering, or architecture, for example, there are plenty of examples where the division has the opportunity to assess other outcome areas through involvement, employment, leadership, and other experiences. Student leaders develop their communication skills as they run meetings, work with their peers, and manage projects. Resident assistants use their communication and critical thinking skills when speaking to their residents, from resolving roommate conflicts to planning programs. Even students who go through the conduct process (hopefully!) develop better critical thinking and decision-making skills. So the challenge to the division and departments is to develop a systematic approach to assessing and documenting these skills.

When units institute an assessment plan, it provides a structure for not only data collection but also using those results to produce continuous improvement. Although some staff think of assessment as an add-on to what they currently do, it really is an opportunity to develop an attitude (and aptitude) for continuous improvement. Assessment planning and reporting also provide professional development experiences for staff.

Very few institutions and divisions have excess money right now. Assessment should coordinate with planning and budgeting decisions. What programs are worth keeping? What programs may have outlived their usefulness? What new programs and services need to be created? What current programs might need a little boost to make them outstanding? How do SSAOs make those decisions as unit heads are asking for more resources? Expecting units to engage in assessment and provide needed information will lead to systematic decision making and appropriate investment of resources. Gene Zdziarski, SSAO at Roanoke College indicated that "only initiatives that are linked to the institutional strategic plan, have a well-developed plan based on sound assessment data, receive additional funding" (personal communication, January 22, 2014). Because staff know this, assessment becomes a high priority.

The SSAO's Role in Assessment Plans and Reports

The SSAO plays a key role in establishing the assessment process and setting priorities. Despite not typically being the person crunching the numbers or writing the report, the SSAO sets the tone and expectations for these reports. Some division leaders like to know in some detail what the assessment results are; others want the one-page summary with the big picture. Directors need to understand what the division leadership wants and needs in order to communicate these priorities within their own departments. As Bill Kibler, former SSAO at Mississippi State University stated, "We incorporated assessment and data-driven decision making and evaluation as a 'way of doing business throughout the Division,'" setting the tone for the expectations for assessment plans and reports (personal communication, January 18, 2014).

In *Building a Culture of Evidence in Student Affairs*, Culp (2012) lists several areas in which SSAOs need to lead and manage to ensure divisions use assessment: budgeting, communication, focus, morale and motivation, planning, resources, results, and structure. In terms of results, for example, the division leadership should link data to major initiatives, as well as establish uniform formats and provide training and tools on how to use those reporting formats. The SSAO and senior staff can keep the assessment process and product at the forefront of the planning and execution of duties. To prevent assessment overload and to keep processes manageable, senior leadership also sets reasonable expectations regarding the amount of assessment that takes place in any given time period. Staff could spend all of their time doing assessment to the detriment of other responsibilities, so leadership needs to shape assessment priorities as a long-term commitment. Because many staff feel pressure to assess everything all the time, leadership can set multiyear expectations that map out a rotation of important topics (e.g., satisfaction, learning, climate, needs, benchmarking, etc.).

On one hand, the division leaders provide the moral support for assessment plans and reports. Staff appreciate recognition for their efforts. That recognition could come in the way of writing letters to staff who are doing/ using assessment (and copying their supervisors) or creating an award to formally celebrate assessment efforts—really, anything that encourages continued use of assessment for improvement. Staff like to know someone at the upper level values their investment of time and energy. SSAOs can take an interest in and support sharing of assessment results.

On the other hand, division leaders also play the accountability enforcer. Ultimately, they provide consequences if their assessment expectations are not met. Although assessment *results* should not be used in personnel evaluations, staff can be evaluated on their *efforts* to do and use assessment. At Mississippi State University, those expectations are incorporated into the performance expectations and evaluation process with department heads (Bill Kibler, personal communication, January 18, 2014). SSAOs play a key role in keeping assessment at the forefront by asking their employees about their assessment efforts and use of results, especially around issues of planning and budgeting. The division leadership should be having conversations on a regular basis about university accountability efforts as well as individual division goal attainment. Staff who are not meeting expectations should be held accountable through the evaluation process.

SSAOs can reiterate the importance of assessment by making decisions using assessment data. They can model the importance of integrating assessment into short- and long-term goals and outcomes. When a staff member brings forth an idea for a new program or service, the supervisor has the responsibility to ask, "What data do you have to support this new initiative over other initiatives in this department/division/campus?" Assessment planning can provide a fair approach in the decision-making process.

The division leadership should incorporate assessment into planning and budgeting cycles. Very few divisions have the luxury of extra money to spend on whims. Because student affairs assessment is relatively new, it may not have been formally included in planning and budgeting processes. As

Jan Winniford, SSAO at Weber State University, admitted, "This is an area where we have room for improvement" (personal communication, January 9, 2014). To address that situation, her department uses assessment data in requests for additional student fee funds and to justify significant budget changes in the next budget cycle. In addition, divisions review their strategic plans, so units can align their assessment plans with the broader goals. A wise department will provide assessment data to support continuing or new programs when asking for budget dollars and completing annual assessment reports.

A shrewd SSAO will view the landscape and provide the resources for staff to meet expectations. On the assessment planning side, that could include training and professional development on campus, at conferences/ institutes, during webinars, or in courses. In addition, in terms of reporting, the SSAO may want to have one person with graphic design skills create a division assessment report and help support departments who may also do an annual report.

In summary, SSAOs set the tone for assessment expectations. They must articulate their needs, provide resources, and hold staff accountable. In the words of Gene Zdziarski, "It [assessment] is something that gains momentum and needs constant attention from the leadership" (personal communication, January 22, 2014). Expectations should balance the need for staff to engage in quality assessment planning with the reality that staff need to implement quality programs and services on a daily basis.

Implementing Assessment Plans and Reports

When a division begins the assessment plan implementation process, it is important to first establish a common language. Busby and Gonzalez Robinson (2012) indicated that a common language allows for better communication and collaboration. When staff have common definitions of assessment terms, the processes become more efficient. A small group of staff (at the university or division level) should be tasked with creating definitions of terms that will be used in the assessment planning and reporting procedures. Those terms could include, but are not limited to, *vision, mission, goals, outcomes, objectives, assessment, direct measures, indirect measures, formative assessment, summative assessment, evidence,* and so on. Note that different texts and accreditation agencies may have different definitions for similar terms. If this process is done at the university level, know that this step could take time and much discussion. Blaisdell and Chamberlain explain more about the power of language when enacting assessment and strategic planning in the next chapter.

There are many options, ranging from low to high tech, when moving to the actual implementation of assessment plans and reports. On the low-tech side, a template can be created in Word or Excel to create a consistent method to collect the needed information. The template could include the name of the unit, vision mission, goals, outcomes, delivery strategies, assessment methods, criteria for success, results, action plans, implementation results, and connections to any division or institutional priorities. Those forms could be submitted to a person, shared network, or online document repository. On the high-tech side, some divisions and institutions have invested in software to collect information in the process, either a purchased product or a homegrown system. These products may have the ability to analyze progress toward unit, division, and university goals; collect supporting documents in a repository; and provide a longitudinal and comprehensive record of progress toward goals, outcomes, and priorities. This can be very useful on a larger scale, especially if the system can be used for accreditation reviews. Examples include WEAVEonline and Campus Labs' Compliance Assist. Before investing in any product, be sure it meets division needs, coordinates with institutional requirements, and satisfies affordability concerns as a long-term investment. Although SSAOs may not be using the purchased product on a daily basis, they do need to be able to access and use it as needed.

At the same time, SSAOs need to offer information in an organized way that represents the work of the division to stakeholders. For some, that means an annual report turned in at the end of the fiscal year. For others, it could be a glossy publication or online document that highlights the achievements of the units. As an example, the University of Albany's Division of Student Success publishes an annual *Student Success Briefing Book* (Office of the SSAO for Student Success, 2013) to highlight its assessment. It not only provides results of what student affairs knows about students, but also highlights each department's mission, current goals, learning outcomes, assessment results, and goals for the next year. The publication, available on its website for anyone to access, tells the story of the division's contribution to student learning and success. Similarly, Mississippi State University publishes its Division of Student Affairs annual report on its website as well as making a few printed copies for the president and cabinet, the departments, and selected others (Bill Kibler, personal communication, January 18, 2014). Kevin Jackson, at Baylor University, provides information to the president and the board of regents and makes an annual presentation to the Division of Student Life (personal communication, January 10, 2014).

No matter what format is used for an assessment plan or report, the SSAO should provide a clear timeline for completion. For assessment plans, particularly if they link to the institution's plans, there may need to be intermediate deadlines. For example, in the beginning of the year (however that is defined), the SSAO might expect goals, outcomes, and delivery methods to be defined. Several months later, the SSAO might want to see the assessment methods and achievement targets. Finally, as the year comes to a close, staff should be completing reports that indicate assessment results and action plans for the next year. Particularly when assessment plans are new, staff need more support from a person, group, or department who can help them succeed and build confidence and competence. At Weber State University, initial department assessment plans are due August 1, midyear updates are due January 15, and annual reports are due June 1 (Jan Winniford, personal communication, January 9, 2014). The university has a web-based reporting system that provides current information to the division leadership team. The leadership team can provide feedback throughout the year and can see progress made toward goals. At Roanoke College, the departments have midyear and end-of-year reports, but the SSAO also receives information throughout the year about particular programs and services (Gene Zdziarski, personal communication, January 22, 2014). Throughout the year, SSAOs should be having conversations with their staff about expectations, progress, and results.

If a division is starting from the very beginning without any expectation or structure, SSAOs should work to develop a simple framework for an assessment plan and set an expectation that each department will assess one program, activity, or service in the upcoming year. To facilitate that goal, SSAOs can instruct departments to set deadlines, provide support, and incorporate those discussions in further meetings and interactions. In addition, SSAOs can encourage departments to pick a program they already know to be successful, so the assessment experience is positive. If there are some basic plans in place already, it may be time to review progress and challenge staff to step up their game, providing evidence of use of data and reviewing the current processes in place.

If assessment has not been part of the culture of a division, the SSAO and her or his leadership team will face organizational change, which may include attitude, capacity, resource allocation, and staffing changes. Staff may consider assessment planning as another fad or another layer of bureaucracy, and they may fear the process because they do not have the background in assessment or fear that they will get in trouble if their program is not perfect. The organization leadership has to decide how to allocate or reallocate funding to support the assessment planning processes, and they have to determine if or how they will hire staff to coordinate the process on a division level.

Assessment teams can provide an important resource as assessment planning gains momentum. Although structures and purposes differ, assessment teams can be a resource and sounding board for staff. Team members may receive additional training and guide processes, with a goal of supporting division staff in their assessment planning and reporting efforts. If assessment processes are new to an organization, the assessment team can include early adopters and interested staff who influence cultural change. Teams could also be created as a representative model, with each unit having one person participating on the team. That model ensures that information is disseminated throughout the organization. As assessment efforts mature, the nature of the team evolves, too.

As Kevin Jackson, SSAO of student life at Baylor University, described, "I believe you have to approach it from an evolutionary as contrasted to a revolutionary mind-set. That is, long-lasting change (change that continues beyond the leader) occurs when you work within the relevant organization conditions to introduce and cultivate ownership for conducting our work in a different way" (personal communication, January 10, 2014). Division leaders use knowledge of their people, structure, and context to develop the right strategies to encourage success.

To operationalize this philosophy, Jackson suggested using the diffusion of information model. The leadership works with staff to establish the need; seek consensus on the importance of addressing the need; and coordinate with a representative group to develop a plan to address the need, allocate resources, and facilitate the steps in the plan. As the plan is implemented, gaps will be identified and resolved. Throughout the process, the leaders should communicate with staff about progress, celebrate advances, and demonstrate how their planning, implementation, assessment, and reporting helps the overall organization achieve its mission, vision, goals, and outcomes (Kevin Jackson, personal communication, January 10, 2014).

Conclusion

As described earlier in the chapter, assessment plans and reports should align with the institutional mission and strategies. Every unit within a division of student affairs should be working toward the division mission and goals. By framing this work in alignment, the division is better able to provide evidence that resources and programs are being used to support the overall institutional mission. Although some faculty may still believe that student affairs does not contribute to student learning, having a quality assessment plan and a clear reporting process will provide strong evidence that a division is a valued part of student success and learning.

In addition, at the institutional level, divisions are being asked to meet tighter budget constraints. Having strong assessment plans and reports will support good use of resources in meeting the institutional mission. Divisions then have the ability to provide evidence of the value of their programs and services that are assessed for effectiveness and efficiency, as well as student learning.

In recent years, accreditation has become an important conversation in the higher education landscape. Even Congress has joined the debate about the cost versus benefit of the current system. Regardless, divisions are expected to contribute to the accreditation process as a key component in student learning and institutional effectiveness. Divisions that have a strong assessment plan aligned with the university mission and goals will have an easier time when the review process occurs. For example, Bill Kibler at Mississippi State University reported that "our division was fully prepared based on an already well-established annual report process that integrated learning based goal setting, assessment and evaluation and assurance that we were in sync with the institutional priorities set forth in the University's strategic plan" (personal communication, January 18, 2014). Mississippi State University's Office of Institutional Research even complimented the Division of Student Affairs for being so well prepared. But having a plan is not enough; accreditors are looking for use of assessment results to make improvements (and then assessment of those changes to ensure they have actually been beneficial). So assessment planning and reports are not a "one and done" effort every 10 years. They have to be incorporated into every aspect of the business we are in.

SSAOs who are beginning the journey of assessment planning and reporting should keep these considerations in mind. We offer the following recommendations:

1. A common language needs to be established early on to enhance communication. It is helpful to know the common language used at the institution level.
2. All of these efforts should align with the institution's directions, processes, and timelines. The division does not operate in a vacuum.
3. The division leaders need to set solid but flexible expectations for participation in the process. They need to be consistent in the message, promote the processes, and hold units accountable for their efforts. It may be hard in the first year of implementation, and the process may need to be adapted and revised.
4. A manageable and meaningful model needs to be developed that includes templates and timeframes. Initially, having a structured plan and report template allows staff to insert the answers, rather than having to also figure out what the questions are. Over time, the templates can be adjusted as needed to provide useful information.

5. There needs to be a process and structure for how information is going to be shared inside and outside of the division. The SSAO needs to know who the stakeholders are and what information is needed by each group.

In summary, SSAOs are the drivers for assessment planning and reporting in their divisions. They set expectations, furnish resources, and make decisions based on information provided. Their leadership can instill a structured assessment process, which is essential for their ability to share information inside and outside of their division. In the next chapter, Blaisdell and Chamberlain look at connecting the divisional assessment plan to the institution's overall strategic plan. They consider how culture and context influence student affairs assessment priorities and how the division can best contribute to the overall goals of the college or university.

References

Bresciani, M. J., Zelna, C. L., & Anderson, J. A. (2004). *Assessing student learning and development: A handbook for practitioners.* Washington, DC: NASPA.

Busby, K., & Gonzalez Robinson, B. (2012). Developing the leadership team to establish and maintain a culture of evidence in student affairs. In M. M. Culp & G. J. Dungy (Eds.), *Building a culture of evidence in student affairs: A guide for leaders and practitioners* (pp. 35–59). Washington, DC: NASPA.

Culp, M. M. (2012). Establishing a culture of evidence foundation. In M. M. Culp & G. J. Dungy (Eds.), *Building a culture of evidence in student affairs: A guide for leaders and practitioners* (pp. 21–34). Washington, DC: NASPA.

Division of Student Affairs. (2014). *Cycle of assessment.* Retrieved from http://saa.gatech.edu/plugins/content/index.php?id=41

Division of Student Affairs and Enrollment Management. (2014a). *FY15 annual planning workbook template.* Retrieved from http://www.niu.edu/stuaff/Planning Assessment/Annual_Planning/FY_Planning/FY15AnnualPlanningWorkbook Template_FINAL_3.4.14.xlsx

Division of Student Affairs and Enrollment Management. (2014b). *2013 annual report.* Retrieved from http://issuu.com/northernillinoisuniversity/docs/2013saem_annualreport_1116

Office of the SSAO for Student Success. (2013). *Student success briefing book.* Retrieved from http://www.albany.edu/studentsuccess/assessment/BriefingBook/Briefing%20Book%202012-13.pdf

Suskie, L. (2009). *Assessing student learning: A common sense guide* (2nd ed.). San Francisco, CA: Jossey-Bass.

Appendix 7.A

Assessment Plan Template

Unit Name:
Vision and Core Values (if applicable):
Mission:
Goals:
Connection to Division and/or Institution Goals/Priorities:
Learning Outcome(s):
> Delivery Method:
Criteria for Success:
Timeline:
> Data Collection Method:
> Analysis Process:
> Results:
> Action Plan:
Program/Process Outcome(s):
Delivery Method:
Criteria for Success:
Timeline:
> Data Collection Method:
> Analysis Process:
> Results:
> Action Plan:

Appendix 7.B

Assessment Report Template

Department Name:
Vision (if applicable):
Mission:
Core Values (if applicable):
Goals:
Outcomes:
Highlights of Results:
Improvements Based on Assessment (could be multiyear period):

8

TENET EIGHT: CONNECT ASSESSMENT PLANS TO INSTITUTIONAL AND DIVISIONAL GOALS

Stephanie Blaisdell and Todd Chamberlain

SSAO's Perspective

Gail DiSabatino

Did you ever watch the lineup in a football game switch almost instantaneously? What you were seeing was the collision of strategic planning and assessment. A team has its plan, rooted in broad goals: block the opponent, score touchdowns, win the game. The plan is based upon many factors that they have learned about through assessment (individual talents, team performance in the past, review of their opponent's performance). They couple this assessment with coaches' and players' ideas, and they plan how the team will execute plays on the field. Then they get to the field and things change—new assessments tell them that the other team is handling things differently or a player is hurt, and so on. Because of their careful, yet flexible, advance planning, they can be nimble and shift to a different approach. The goals are still the same—block the opponent, score touchdowns, win the game.

Football fans may be laughing themselves silly at my simplistic description of the game. Yet I propose that there are similarities to our work in student affairs and the benefits of integrating strategic planning and assessment. We each have established goals for our divisions—maybe as simple as nurturing students to learn and succeed. Most of us are doing assessment. What I have learned over the years is that if we don't use our assessments to make adjustments to our plans, we reduce the likelihood that we will achieve our goals, and our credibility with stakeholders will diminish. Winning teams develop plans based on overarching goals and preliminary assessment, conduct assessment based on the plan, and use their ongoing assessments to make continuous changes to the plans.

As the coach, the senior student affairs officer (SSAO) must clarify goals and establish expectations for developing strategic plans and assessment. We must promote transparency for using the assessment to change the plan, and we need to celebrate the outcomes. One of the greatest challenges will occur when something in the plan doesn't work—you may find resistance to changing the plan. Let your staff know that it is okay to fail, as long as they learn something and make adjustments (after all, isn't this what we teach our students?). Reward the change makers! Developing robust strategic plans that are accompanied by and integrated with meaningful assessment will give us a win for our most important stakeholders—our students.

Linking Assessment Plans to Institutional and Divisional Strategic Plans

Why link assessment with strategic planning? Simply put, because strategic planning sets priorities for organizational outcomes, and assessment maps both the starting point and checkpoints toward those outcomes. Assessment has little value when it is disconnected from a shared framework for divisional values and priorities. Strategic planning falters without structured, evidence-based mechanisms for evaluating whether changes to educational environments and student learning experiences are effectively achieving desired results.

At its core, strategic planning seeks to ensure that people, facilities, capital, and other resources are deployed to most effectively support student success in ways that are valued at your institution. Done properly, strategic planning processes will:

- clarify division of student affairs priorities in ways that are not only clearly understood by internal and external stakeholders but also appropriately flexible in enabling individual units to interpret how those priorities relate to their functional areas,
- enable resource prioritization in the face of limited time and resources;
- identify performance gaps for both the division and individual units, and
- provide a shared framework to identify potential redundancies or opportunities for collaboration between units within and outside the division.

Successfully integrated planning and assessment processes require broad ownership and participation at all levels of an organization, but the SSAO plays a pivotal role in creating a vision for what the division's future should look like and setting expectations for evidence-based decision making guided by standards developed as part of the planning process. This chapter provides an overview of theoretical models of organizational change to consider when developing a strategic planning process; establishes the role of the SSAO in strategic planning; outlines the language of strategic planning; and details important considerations in developing and implementing a strategic, assessment-based approach to organizational improvement.

Models for Organizational Change

At its core, *student affairs strategic planning emanates from a desire to change organizational conditions to improve the quality of educational environments and experiences for students.* No matter how well a student affairs division operates, areas for improvement always remain, such as students whose needs are not met, missed opportunities for student learning, and ways to use resources more effectively.

A basic understanding of organizational theory helps the SSAO and key student affairs staff discern how characteristics of their particular institutional and organizational context will shape the nature of their strategic planning process. Change in higher education is typically characterized as incremental rather than transformational, although factors sometimes emerge that stimulate rapid and significant organizational change (Bess & Dee, 2008). Changing conditions internal and external to the organization guarantee that change will eventually occur, whether quickly or slowly. The role of the SSAO is to foster development of conditions that intentionally move change in a direction that creates a better experience for students.

As noted by Bennis, Benne, and Chin, models of change based on a *planned change* framework conceptualize change as "an intentional effort to improve organizational processes through the implementation of new ideas based on scientific knowledge" (as cited in Bess & Dee, 2008, p. 797). Planned change models assume a more centralized, hierarchical organizational structure in which change is directed from higher levels of management. Within institutions of higher education, this approach may be more effective at smaller institutions where student affairs organizational structures are less complex and practitioner roles are more generalized. Planned change models still involve collaboration and consensus building, but they assume a greater potential for developing a tightly defined idea of what improvement looks like across the entire organization.

Higher education institutions are more commonly characterized as loosely coupled, meaning they comprise multiple subunits that operate with a high degree of autonomy and varied perspectives within a shared organizational framework (Orton & Weick, 1990). SSAOs should consider how the varied needs of different departments might benefit from higher or lower levels of coupling in their operations and planning. For example, since the 1970s, a recognition of the related roles of admissions, registrar, and financial aid has led to the development of enrollment management models to foster greater integration (i.e., tighter coupling) of these functional areas, and hence some loss of autonomy of the individual functions in matters of strategic planning and quality improvement initiatives. At Clemson University, strategic planning is a division-wide process that considers how all departments contribute to student affairs goals, but departments have been organizationally clustered based on shared priorities and given some latitude to develop planning initiatives that address their particular emphasis areas.

To illustrate, the career center, health center, counseling center, and judicial affairs unit, as well as new student and family programs, all report to the dean of students in order to align efforts focused on student care and concerns. Changes made within any of these units are more closely considered for their impact on other division departments. For example, although the Clemson University fire department and police department collaborate regularly with departments in the dean of students area, strategic planning processes for fire and police are less tightly coupled with the dean of students area, because fire and police get much of their direction from national and state standards for their profession while still remaining attentive to considerations unique to Clemson.

Emergent change models have developed to account for loosely coupled organizations by recognizing that subunits within the larger organization are constantly adapting to the specific conditions of their context, regardless of guidance from higher levels of administration. Rather than simply imposing a centralized vision, the role of the SSAO is to "identify unifying patterns and themes in the organization's dispersed grassroots initiatives and then provide the recognition and support necessary" (Bess & Dee, 2008, p. 798) to implement those initiatives division-wide. In an emergent change model, assessment provides not only independent guidance for quality improvement *within* individual departments, but also source information for a meta-analysis of trends *across* the division. In a recent example at Clemson University, a staff member in new student programs who began exploring ways to better serve student veterans found that multiple departments across the university were wrestling with related issues. This led to a collaborative group that is developing solutions for staff training and specialized services to deal with the unique needs of these students, and these needs are now being incorporated into planning initiatives for the division.

As noted by Birnbaum (1988), organizational realities of a specific institution rarely fit neatly into the distinct models developed by theorists to make sense of complex organizational dynamics, but they do provide a guide to prevalent patterns that can influence how one approaches organizational leadership and change. At Clemson, much of our planning and assessment are grounded in a planned change model coordinated at the divisional level, but as with the example of student veterans referenced previously, organizational culture also allows for the incorporation of priorities that emerge from individual departments. Planned change and emergent change models may be compatible within the same institution at different times and within different contexts, and savvy leaders learn to distinguish when each will be most effective.

The SSAO's Role in Strategic Planning

The SSAO's role in strategic planning centers on ensuring that student affairs initiatives align with the institution's strategic planning priorities. Especially at larger institutions, an effective model of planning and assessment cannot solely be managed by SSAOs, but they do bear the responsibility for understanding overall institutional context and creating conditions that foster a collaborative environment in which units with varying functions can work together toward shared outcomes.

The SSAO's first priority is to understand the university's strategic plan and the role of student affairs within it. The institutional strategic plan may include elements that explicitly spell out expectations for student affairs, but other times the SSAO needs to interpret the specific ways the division can contribute to the success of the strategic plan, and how it will be held accountable. SSAOs can also play a role in helping other university administrators see how student affairs can support the university's objectives. By designing assessments that demonstrate how student affairs contributes to the stated outcomes (e.g., increased retention and graduation, improved student learning, engaging all students), student affairs can build an evidence-based case for its value in supporting the university's priorities, as well as a plan for continued improvement.

The Language of Strategic Planning

Strategic planning has a vocabulary all its own, and understanding the basics is an important first step in connecting it with assessment. Universities may differ in the terms they use, but it is critical that everyone within the institution use the same terms. In *Managing the Big Picture* (Alfred, 2006), three layers of strategic planning are outlined: declarations, tactics, and strategies.

Declarations are defined as "statements that make a college's intentions known regarding its purpose and nature of its business" (p. 11). Examples of declarations are the mission and vision statements. While declarations create a foundation, they are meaningless without tactics and strategies to operationalize them and to help members across the institution identify a role in supporting them.

Alfred (2006) defines *tactics* as "the means a college will employ to achieve its mission" (p. 13) with a short-term focus. *Strategies* have a longer-term focus and help to differentiate institutions by uniquely qualifying how each will pursue its goals. Similarly, at the University of Memphis, our strategic planning vocabulary includes tactics that support strategies; however, we use the term *actions as* an additional layer between the two. A glossary of our planning language is in Table 8.1.

Again, there are no right or wrong uses of terminology as long as everyone at the institution uses terms in the same manner. The point is to know in which direction the university is heading, what role the division of student affairs plays in helping it move, and what to do to connect each department—and each staff member—to their ownership of success.

Setting a Course: The Role of Vision and Mission

Mission statements may be one of the first things people think about when they consider the elements of planning, but critiques include the tendency of mission statements to be so generic that they provide little practical understanding of how to prioritize organizational efforts, and also that they tend to be something written and then forgotten in the context of regular planning exercises. In their study of high-performing institutions, Kuh, Kinzie, Schuh, Whitt, and associates (2005) identified the importance of institutions aligning their espoused and enacted mission statements. The power of a mission statement comes from its potential to encapsulate in very simple ways what an institution is and what it wants to be and do. Powerful mission statements do this in a way that is easy to understand internally and externally, while also providing some flexibility in interpretation by diverse operational units within the overall organization.

Although mission statements may include an aspirational component, one way to create a distinction between what the organization does and what it wants to be is by stating a distinct vision and mission statement. At Clemson, our student affairs vision statement is explicitly linked to our university vision: "Clemson University's vision is to become a top-20 institution. In support of this vision, Student Affairs will provide an exemplary,

TABLE 8.1
University of Memphis Strategic Planning Terminology

	Term	One Definition	Example
What we want to accomplish	Vision	A compelling description of how the organization will or should be at some point in the future	The University of Memphis will be recognized as one of America's great metropolitan research universities.
	Goals	Broad statements of what the university plans to achieve	Student success: Provide superior learning experiences for students built on strong academic programs, and so on.
What we will do to get there	Strategies	Broad, overarching efforts to be undertaken to achieve the university goals	Recruit academically qualified students who reflect the geographic, cultural, disciplinary, and quality goals of a superior metropolitan research university.
	Objectives	Measurable steps toward accomplishment of strategy	Develop standards and programs targeting academically high-ability students.
	Actions (mainly at division level)	Specific actions that will be undertaken to accomplish the strategies or objectives and demonstrate progress toward the goals	Structure the scholarship program to recruit high-ability students and National Merit Scholars.
How we will know if we are making progress	Strategic measures	Evidence of achievement of the goals	Percentage of undergraduate students enrolled in the honors program.

comprehensive, and integrated student life curriculum, resulting in the nation's most engaged, satisfied, and successful student body" (Clemson University Division of Student Affairs, 2015). As described by Collins (2001, p. 93) this is our "big, hairy, audacious goal," which sets the bar for the level of excellence we seek to achieve within our particular niche of higher education. As established by our mission statement, we pursue this vision by creating "supportive environments and innovative opportunities for student learning." Underpinning all of this is the division-wide value that we believe each person has the power to positively impact the world, and our ultimate outcome for students is that their Clemson experience better prepares them to enable this positive impact.

At the University of Memphis, the student affairs mission is "to foster student learning and promote student success through engagement and involvement in community, academics, diversity, and leadership" (University of Memphis Division of Student Affairs, 2015). This is in support of the university's mission to be a "learner-centered metropolitan research university providing high quality educational experiences while pursuing new knowledge through research, artistic expression, and interdisciplinary and engaged scholarship" (University of Memphis, 2015). However, as our SSAO will readily tell you, while no one in the division of student affairs can tell you our mission, they can easily recite our motto: "Students learning through engagement and involvement" (University of Memphis, 2015).

Ideally, mission statements are developed through an interactive process in which a broad range of organizational constituents discover the priorities already implicit in their work, rather than artificially designating a framework that is not meaningful.

Connecting Student Affairs to the University Strategic Plan: An Example

Goals for the University of Memphis include student success, research and creativity, access and diversity, partnerships, campus culture and service excellence, and sense of place. The division of student affairs has a role in each of these, but it is at the next layer, the strategy level, that it becomes clear how the division can provide leadership. Strategies supporting the University of Memphis's goal of student success, for example, include the following:

1. Offer academic programming that successfully increases student learning.
2. Increase and promote academic programming that critically engages cultural/social/intercultural differences.
3. Increase student persistence and timely graduation.
4. Increase educational experience through regional, national, and international engagement.

5. Strengthen student connections to the university community.
6. Emphasize learning experiences that develop students and alumni into leaders in their professions and communities.

Student affairs adopted strategies 3 and 5 as our division goals.

Actions are agreed upon at the institutional level; however, they begin to more precisely represent how specific departments' contributions will allow the institution to achieve the strategy and ultimately the goal. The division of student affairs identified a number of institutional actions for which we could provide leadership. In effect, the institution's actions are student affairs's strategies.

Strengthening student connections to the university community (strategy 5) requires leadership from student affairs. Actions supporting this strategy include the following:

• Create and promote outdoor and intramural activities that meet the needs of all students.
• Increase the variety of on campus venues in which student affairs programs are promoted and offered.
• Increase the number of students living on campus.
• Develop services for extended programs that connect students.
• Partner with academic units to promote experiential learning opportunities.
• Partner with athletics to create a sense of excitement around athletic events.

Using these and other actions as a guide, student affairs departments then adopt tactics each year that will contribute to the success of the action, and ultimately the strategy. Identifying strategies, objectives, and actions requires a fundamental understanding of the institution's goals, as well as a current analysis of the strengths, weaknesses, opportunities, and threats to the division.

SWOT Analysis: Exploring Organizational Identity and External Conditions

Developed in the 1960s and 1970s at the Stanford Research Institute (Humphrey, 2005), strengths, weaknesses, opportunities, and threats (SWOT) analysis is an environmental scanning and organizational planning tool originally developed from business research and later applied to higher education by George Keller (1983). By using this framework, organizations are able to identify (a) current areas of strength and weakness; (b) opportunities for growth, development, or improvement; and (c) internal and external threats to success as a starting point for strategic planning. A SWOT process develops a realistic understanding of an organization's current state and identifies where attention should be focused in order to achieve its idealized future as laid out in the vision.

A wide range of information (finance, market analysis, reviews of organizational culture and climate, skills and interests of staff members, etc.) should be consulted when developing a comprehensive SWOT analysis, which is most valuable at the early stages of a strategic planning process. To foster greater investment in the process and commitment to the results of the SWOT analysis, participation across multiple departments and at different levels of the institutional hierarchy should be involved in the data-gathering and review stages. Possible data sources include nationally normed surveys as well as locally developed surveys that collect information about institutional experiences of current students, alumni, staff, and administrators. Focus groups and other qualitative methods can add richness and context to make meaning out of the quantitative results.

Morrill (2007) offers the caution that SWOT processes can inadvertently veer more strongly in the direction of negativity and suggests the need to move conversations about weaknesses toward an examination of root causes rather than dwelling on symptoms. The final objective of a SWOT process is to identify how areas in which the organization performs well can be adapted to meet unmet needs and correct or move away from lower performing areas. For example, one possible solution to chronic problems with an institutionally administered food services program may be to decide that organizational needs are better met by outsourcing food services and focusing more energy on strengthening the quality of residential life programs that only need minor tweaking.

Decisions About Measurement and Data Management

Assessment, such as the SWOT analysis described previously, drives the creation of the strategic plan. Assessment allows a division of student affairs to prioritize what it wants to increase or improve. Assessing progress once the strategic plan is established is equally important.

With each level supporting the other, it may seem sufficient to measure progress at the top, by assessing goals. This is what we had historically done at the University of Memphis. However, we know that *what* is measured matters. We tend to pay less attention to things for which we are not held accountable. Without accountability at the more specific levels of the strategic plan, there can be no movement at the top. Also, measuring the effectiveness and outcomes of tactics and actions helps to account for any movement at the strategy and goal level. If there is improvement in student persistence and graduation rates, yet no significant increase for the actions supporting that strategy, or progress at the action level but no movement at the strategy level, there is a misalignment between the two and it is time to reevaluate the plan. Therefore, it is important to assess not only each level, but also the relationships between them.

Assessing each level requires different approaches. Assessing at higher levels will inherently cover a broader sweep of information. Dashboards are often utilized at these levels to indicate movement in the aggregated data. Dashboards can provide a quick visual representation of current data in light of the baseline and the goal. Assessing at more specific levels will require more tailored approaches based on the nature of the action or tactic.

Managing the flow of assessment data from the smallest organizational units up through higher levels of the organization presents a challenge, which can be mitigated through technology. For smaller institutions, spreadsheets may be sufficient for compiling information that shows how departmental, divisional, and institutional results interrelate. Larger institutions, however, may require a more robust database system that can manage multiple relationships among data inputs and help distribute data-management workload across the division.

Some institutions develop in-house solutions, but many universities use third-party vendors that have created database software specifically geared toward educational assessment or accreditation. A full discussion of technology options is beyond the scope of this chapter (for strategic plan tracking, the University of Memphis uses TracDat and Clemson University uses WEAVE, but there are a number of other vendors), but SSAOs should consider many factors when evaluating options.

A primary consideration is whether there is already a university software system in place to manage assessment and accreditation processes. In this case, the SSAO may have little ability to choose if university policy dictates the use of one system institution-wide, but the SSAO might also be able to make a case that unique factors within the division of student affairs justify a different software choice if it continues to achieve university requirements.

Although the prioritization of other factors may vary among institutions, a secondary consideration is ease of use for entering data into the system. One of the key advantages of any technology solution should be the ability to distribute workload so that the smallest organizational units can easily enter their own assessment and planning data directly into the system, and then have their entries easily aggregated at higher organizational levels, up to the university level. Database systems can be notoriously challenging to manage, though, and an interface that is intuitive for those who may not be technologically savvy will help increase its proper use.

A tertiary consideration is whether there is value in software that integrates with other campus data systems. For example, campuses that use software to manage student organization records might want to automate the flow of analytics (e.g., number of organizations, event attendance, etc.) from that software into the assessment tracking software. Integrating technology in this way may require more work up front but helps avoid redundant data entry or inconsistent reports.

A quaternary consideration is the reporting capacity of the software. Such software should be able to generate high-level summaries of progress toward organizational objectives as well as more detailed reports about the assessment data that support these reports. Ideally, a software package will include the capacity to visualize progress in a dashboard-type fashion that is easily digestible by multiple audiences.

When set up and managed properly, good assessment and planning tracking software allows data to be fed into the system so that they can be viewed across departments and breaks out different components of a strategic plan, such as findings that relate to a specific objective. Knowing your department's contribution to a university's Action is easily accessible by the president's office provides an additional level of accountability often accompanied by a higher sense of urgency and responsiveness by staff. Both the University of Memphis and Clemson University used our respective systems for Southern Association of Colleges and Schools Commission on Colleges reaccreditation documents, which proved to be an efficient means to demonstrate how student affairs has responded to assessment data and shaped goals over time.

Although university-wide data systems are useful, there can be challenges as well. It may be difficult to balance the factors discussed previously, and there are cost considerations as well, so compromises may be necessary. Any type of software solution requires training, and there may be pushback from less technologically savvy users. It is necessary to have at least one point person within a division to provide instruction and support. The division point person should have sufficient in-house access to make changes within the system and direct access to the vendor for technical support.

Fostering Collaboration and Integrated Planning

As far back as *The Student Personnel Point of View* (American Council on Education, 1937, 1949), student affairs leaders have asserted the need for collaborative planning and policy making that includes professionals from all functional areas and varied levels of the organizational hierarchy. The loose coupling of units within an organization described earlier is not necessarily a negative trait (e.g., some degree of independent operation can foster nimbler responses to factors that affect only one unit of the organization), but excessive independent planning within a student affairs division can also stifle collaboration and allow development of wasteful service redundancies or blind spots that leave student needs unmet. Properly shared and strategically directed, assessment data can provide a common body of knowledge that identifies student needs and provides a framework for collaboration toward common priorities.

Despite consistent calls for educational collaboration, however, organizational silos often inhibit the kinds of cooperative partnerships needed to maximize student learning (American Association for Higher Education, American College Personnel Association, & National Association of Student Personnel Administrators, 1998; American College Personnel Association, 1996; Kuh, 1996; Kuh et al., 2005), foster innovation (Dungy & Ellis, 2011), and effectively serve diverse student needs in a climate of tighter finances and greater accountability (Kuk, Banning, & Amey, 2010; Manning, Kinzie, & Schuh, 2006; Moneta & Jackson, 2011). Culp and Dungy (2012) concluded that building a culture of evidence supporting student learning and organizational effectiveness requires assessment capacity among division leadership as well as collaborative teams crossing departmental and divisional lines.

One approach that Clemson University has adopted to increase coordinated progress toward division of student affairs priorities has been the creation of interdepartmental teams assigned to each one of the division's six strategic goals. These groups were tasked with reviewing assessment data related to their goal, identifying key performance indicators, and tracking progress toward specific objectives within each goal.

This team-based approach has been very effective in promoting a shared language around assessment and building partnerships across departments in relation to each of Clemson's six divisional goals. A monthly meeting of the chairs and other leaders for each goal team has also fostered strong working relationships and sharing of ideas across the six goals. The next phase of development for these teams will be greater emphasis on developing specific action plans and more proactive interaction between the goal teams and departments to develop responses to unmet objectives.

Collaborative teams that advance planning and assessment can take many forms and serve different purposes, but organizations seeking to build effective collaborative structures should focus on some core general principles:

- *Clear purpose or outcome expectation.* A topical focus (e.g., commuter students, leadership learning, etc.) may be a starting point, but

progress will be slow unless the group is clear about what they are
expected to accomplish.

- *Broad representation by the right people.* Members of collaborative
  teams need to include people who represent diverse perspectives on
  the problem and those who are able to implement proposed changes.
- *Role clarity.* Each team member should be clear about how his or her
  participation is expected to advance the process.
- *Open communication.* Team members must openly express their
  perspectives while being open to other viewpoints and solutions.
- *Explicit mechanisms for enacting the planning and assessment proposals
  developed by the team.* It should be clear from the outset who will
  review and approve work developed by the team so that strategies can
  be enacted.

Reporting Cycles and Processes

The many individual layers of assessment within the overall strategic plan of
departmental or institutional assessment can become cumbersome. One mechanism for managing the data is to establish checkpoints in time (see Chapter
7 for a more in-depth discussion of the assessment cycle). At the University of
Memphis, our student affairs planning cycle begins with loading information
into TracDat in November or early December for the following academic year.
Those data are to be reviewed by each department's respective assistant vice
president and then the student affairs leadership group. Each department then
presents its plan in December and January. Presentations are open to other
student affairs departments and to key staff and faculty from other divisions,
providing excellent communication and feedback opportunities. Departments
revise their plans based on feedback gleaned through the planning meeting process. The January timeline is driven by university deadlines including budget
revisions for the next fiscal year. Over the summer, when assessment data from
the current academic year have been analyzed, departments are encouraged to
revisit their plans for further revisions. Once the new academic year begins,
plans are static. The following summer, assessment data and progress reports
are due into TracDat. Explanations are expected for any plans not undertaken,
and there is an opportunity to report on any new plans adopted that had not
been anticipated. Collectively, these data are communicated through internal
and external annual reports. The annual reports and the data as entered into
TracDat are viewable by the leadership across the institution.

Organizational Culture

SSAOs must consider their organizational culture when devising an approach
to strategic planning. As evidenced previously, student affairs strategic

planning at the University of Memphis now flows seamlessly from and to the institution's strategic plan. In fact, student affairs has provided leadership to the institution on strategic planning as the division's system was by and large adopted by the institution. The division's timing of planning meetings was dictated by the institution's budget cycle; plans requiring additional resources were presented prior to budgetary deadlines.

Some institutions already have a culture of assessment. Where formal assessment is not highly valued by an institution's administration, a division of student affairs can still cultivate a culture of assessment. Even when not immediately valued outside of the division, a culture of assessment provides continual feedback for improvement; marks progress in adherence to Council for the Advancement of Standards (CAS) guidelines and other benchmarking; and allows opportunities for staff professional development, presentations, and publications.

Interestingly, at the writing of this chapter, both authors' institutions were in the midst of leadership transitions. At the University of Memphis, there had been a number of administrative and resource adjustments. Our new president and new provost both indicated that attention to providing data allowed our division to retain programs, and perhaps even to expand in a time of scarcity. Clemson University has also recently secured a new president and provost. Although the general tone of transition has been continued, commitment to the current university strategic plan as well as specific emphases within the plan may shift as these leaders learn more about the institution. As noted earlier, change is inevitable, so the implication for planning is to be prepared with assessment data that could inform responses to new expectations or priorities.

SSAOs also must determine the most effective management of a strategic plan in light of organizational culture, including attitudes toward technology. At both the University of Memphis and Clemson University, we have received some negative feedback about current and past data management systems. This is likely a combination of a general dislike of technology by some directors and the lack of simplicity in our systems in other cases. At Clemson we are working to consolidate some redundant reporting processes so that information can be synthesized multiple ways for different audiences. However, when the message is clear that strategic planning and assessment are highly valued, dislike is tolerated and the ultimate goal is achieved. Of course, it helps to be empathetic and to have a commitment to an ever-evolving process that emphasizes quality improvement outcomes over rigid adherence to process for its own sake.

Conclusion

An effective strategic plan keeps a student affairs division dynamic. Our students' needs are always evolving, and we must continue to change in response. Universities are facing unprecedented challenges and are responding in creative, innovative ways; moreover, student affairs must be responsive to global, as well as local, paradigm shifts. Strategic planning is inherently based on the continual assessment of both internal and external environments and processes. Documenting student affairs's role within and contributions to the institution through strategic planning is a critical function of the SSAO.

In conclusion, we recommend the following:

1. Know the university's strategic plan and student affairs's role within it.
2. Ensure that you are speaking the same strategic planning language as the rest of the campus.
3. Conduct a SWOT analysis within student affairs as it relates to the strategic plan.
4. Create a plan for improved support of the university's priorities and design assessment that measures student affairs's contribution.
5. Communicate the plan and the data to the rest of the university.

These recommendations can help divisions of student affairs enact a culture where planning and assessment are interconnected. When these processes are interconnected we provide evidence of how student affairs programs, resources, and services contribute to the larger institution mission, vision, and strategies. Such evidence must come in many forms to tell the student affairs story. In the next chapter, Wise provides an overview of how student affairs can tell its story through varied assessment methods.

References

Alfred, R. L. (2006). *Managing the big picture*. Westport, CT: Praeger.

American Association for Higher Education, American College Personnel Association, & National Association of Student Personnel Administrators. (1998). *Powerful partnerships: A shared responsibility for learning*. Washington, DC: Authors.

American College Personnel Association. (1996). *The student learning imperative: Implications for student affairs*. Washington, DC: Author.

American Council on Education. (1937). *The student personnel point of view*. Washington, DC: Author.

American Council on Education. (1949). *The student personnel point of view*. Washington, DC: Author.

Bess, J. L., & Dee, J. R. (2008). *Understanding college and university organization: Theories for effective policy and practice*. Sterling, VA: Stylus.

Birnbaum, R. (1988). *How colleges work: The cybernetics of academic organization and leadership.* San Francisco, CA: Jossey-Bass.

Clemson University Division of Student Affairs. (2015). *Vision.* Retrieved from http://www.clemson.edu/administration/student-affairs/vision.html

Collins, J. (2001). *Good to great: Why some companies make the leap . . . and others don't.* New York, NY: Harper Business.

Culp, M. M., & Dungy, G. J. (2012). *Building a culture of evidence in student affairs: A guide for leaders and practitioners.* Washington, DC: NASPA.

Dungy, G. J., & Ellis, G. J. (2011). *Exceptional senior student affairs administrators' leadership: Strategies and competencies for success.* Washington, DC: NASPA.

Humphrey, A. (2005, December). SWOT analysis for management consulting. *SRI Alumni Newsletter, 7–8.*

Keller, G. (1983). *Academic strategy: The management revolution in American higher education.* Baltimore, MD: Johns Hopkins University Press.

Kuh, G. D. (1996). Guiding principles of creating seamless learning environments for undergraduates. *Journal of College Student Development 37*(2), 135–48.

Kuh, G. D., Kinzie, J., Schuh, J. H., Whitt, E. J., & Associates. (2005). *Student success in college: Creating conditions that matter.* San Francisco, CA: Jossey-Bass.

Kuk, L., Banning, J. H., & Amey, M. J. (2010). *Positioning student affairs for sustainable change: Achieving organizational effectiveness through multiple perspectives.* Sterling, VA: Stylus.

Manning, K., Kinzie, J., & Schuh, J. (2006). *One size does not fit all: Traditional and innovative models of student affairs practice.* New York, NY: Routledge.

Moneta, L., & Jackson, M. L. (2011). The new world of student affairs. In G. J. Dungy & S. E. Ellis (Eds.), *Exceptional senior student affairs administrators' leadership: Strategies and competencies for success.* Washington, DC: NASPA.

Morrill, R. L. (2007). *Strategic leadership: Integrating strategy and leadership in colleges and universities.* Lanham, MD: Rowman & Littlefield.

Orton, J. D., & Weick, K. E. (1990). Loosely coupled systems: A reconceptualization. *Academy of Management Review, 15*(2), 203–223.

University of Memphis. (2015). *Strategic plan.* Retrieved from http://www.memphis.edu/presweb/stratplan/index.php

University of Memphis Division of Student Affairs. (2015). *Mission and goals.* Retrieved from http://www.memphis.edu/studentaffairs/about/mission.php

9

TENET NINE: DETERMINE THE APPROPRIATE METHODS FOR ASSESSING PROGRAMS AND SERVICES

Vicki L. Wise

SSAO's Perspective

Dan Fortmiller

Stakeholders, both internal and external to universities, are questioning issues of educational quality, student accessibility, and affordability. According to the Educational Advisory Board, "Given the current economic situation, institutions are being forced to take a hard look at services, facilities, and budgets and evaluate what can be cut or scaled back" (Student Affairs Leadership Council, 2009, p. 5). It is in this climate that universities are asked to be even more transparent in their practices and to provide evidence of institutional effectiveness and impact on student learning. Universities that are poised to demonstrate impact are the most likely to survive these challenging times.

Unfortunately, in times of budget cuts some stakeholders may view the student affairs portfolio, in part, as nonessential to student learning. Divisions of student affairs that have created a culture of accountability and use data to inform decision making will be better poised to demonstrate to stakeholders how they meet the institutional mission and make a difference in student learning. By this time in this book we hope you have realized this demand.

It is upon the leadership of the senior student affairs officer (SSAO) and her or his team to create a place for building a culture of assessment where evidence-based decision making is valued: "It is the responsibility of the chief student affairs officer to address the organizational barriers to strong assessment by: creating clear expectations around assessment for all staff, investing resources to support staff assessment efforts, and holding staff accountable for the quality of their assessment plan/results" (Student Affairs Leadership Council, 2009, p. 6). Moreover, by building a culture of evidence student affairs can "document with hard data the significant contributions student affairs makes toward the institution's mission and goals" (Culp, 2012, p. 1).

However, not all assessment evidence is equal and some methods provide more robust measures of impact on student learning. Robust data provide evidence that we are meeting the institutional mission, vision, and goals and that we are shown to be accurate and comprehensive while directly measuring impacts on student learning. The SSAO must set the tone for collecting and using robust data gleaned from diverse methods that properly answer the question we need to answer. That is the focus of this chapter.

SSAOs must expect their units to share data, to tell their stories of their collective impact on students, and this sharing of data needs to occur both internal and external to the university. When stakeholders question the worth and value of a degree, given the financial costs to students and their families, they need not think of student affairs as an auxiliary set of services. We are making a difference with students; we see it every day. Because of this, we are well poised to share evidence of our impact.

Previous chapters have emphasized the importance of demonstrating to our stakeholders the impact of student affairs on the total student experience, including student retention, persistence, and learning. This chapter provides leaders with an overview of methods available to support assessment that can yield credible evidence of the impact of programs and services on students, specifically learning. Content focuses on helping readers better understand qualitative and quantitative assessment methods and the kinds of evidence each provides as well as how to combine methods for a stronger assessment approach.

What to Assess?

As stated in previous chapters, the assessment process does not begin by selecting an assessment tool. It begins with clarifying intention and determining what it is you wish to know. Once you know your questions, you are then able to determine the methods you will use to collect your answers. For example, are you interested in students' satisfaction with a service or an activity, students' learning from participating in an activity, or students' changing behaviors or attitudes because of participation? The answers to these questions will direct you in determining all the ways to gather the best evidence. The most appropriate method for gathering evidence might be tracking student usage; reviewing existing documents and data; or noting findings from sources such as focus groups or interviews, observations, portfolios, or performance assessments.

Before you get too deep into any assessment method, it is important to determine what priorities you have for assessment in your programs. Not everything has equal value for all assessment purposes. When deciding which programs and services to assess, please consider the following list (Wise & Barham, 2012):

1. *Length of intervention.* When measuring a program's impact, typically, the longer the intervention, the greater the likelihood of achieving hoped-for outcomes, especially learning outcomes. For example, if a desired outcome is to increase student leadership skills, then a program lasting one day has a greater likelihood of increasing these skills than a program lasting only two hours.
2. *Number of participants.* All things being equal, if you have the same program, one with 10 participants and another with 100 participants, then assessment of the larger program is recommended.
3. *Cost/benefit ratio.* If you have programs and services that are particularly costly to implement (in terms of staffing, materials, time, etc.), then you would first want to assess those programs to ensure that resources are being used most appropriately and that you are getting the best return on your investment.
4. *Time and effort invested.* There are very real differences in the investment we make in assessment when we select quantitative or qualitative assessment methods. Quantitative data collection typically involves a larger number of participants, offers greater efficiency with shorter duration, and provides more breadth than depth, whereas qualitative data collection typically involves a smaller number of participants, offers less efficiency with longer duration, and provides more depth than breadth.

Now that you have considered the conditions under which assessment occurs, the resources available, and the potential impact the program can make, we can explore what different types of assessment methods have to offer.

Determining Approaches

To begin with, it is imperative to select methods that are efficient and accurately allow staff to measure the achievement of department-level goals and outcomes. Staff can elect to collect direct and/or indirect evidence to measure outcomes. When measuring student learning, the most robust assessment methods provide direct evidence. Direct evidence requires that students display knowledge, behaviors, and skills. Indirect evidence, on the other hand, relies on students' self-report of what they have learned. This is a less reliable measure and more appropriate for measuring activities where student satisfaction is more important than student learning outcomes, although measuring students' perceptions of their learning is at least better than not measuring at all.

Selecting Assessment Tools

I advocate the use of multiple or mixed methods (more than one form of assessment), as such an approach will provide more valid evidence of the impact of programs and services. To select the right assessment tool, staff need to determine the purpose and intended impact of their programs and services: Why does this program exist? What is its purpose? Then, they need to determine how they will know their programs made an impact and what that evidence would be. When staff answer these questions, selecting the right assessment tool becomes much easier.

Qualitative or quantitative assessment methods or a combination of both, as in mixed methods, can be used to measure student learning, satisfaction, engagement, retention, and persistence. Direct measures include interviews, direct observations, document analysis, tests or quizzes, and rubrics used to evaluate other students' products and performances. Indirect measures include surveys, interviews, rubrics, journals, documents, and university metrics.

Direct Evidence

Interviews. In this procedure, the interviewer uses open-ended questions to elicit views and opinions from students either face-to-face, by telephone, or in a focus group setting. This is a direct assessment if students are asked questions that allow them to provide evidence of learning. Interviews are then analyzed to look for themes or accurate answers. If the questions asked elicit evidence about the achievement of the outcomes intended for the program, then the themes are interpreted in light of this evidence, and program content and delivery modified accordingly. Interviews can be used in conjunction with a survey to further explore students' responses, or they can be used to assist in the development of a survey instrument to learn from a larger sample than those who were initially interviewed.

Observations. Using this method, staff take field notes on the behavior and activities of students in their natural setting or as they participate in an event. Often, but not always, an observational checklist is used to record activities observed at the site. Staff members' levels of participation can range from complete observer to complete participant. Staff members record their observations and interpretations of what is occurring and relate these back to their program goals/objectives. The strength and validity of observational data are increased when paired with another assessment method. If a staff member observes a particular set of behaviors, it may not be possible to know why the behaviors occurred unless student interviews are included. Results can then be interpreted in light of observed behaviors and students' perceptions of what was observed.

Document Analysis. Staff review documents ranging from personal correspondence to official public documents. This method is often used when background/historical information is needed. Document review includes noting the purpose of documents as well as when and for what purpose documents were created. The review can also include assessing the document against specific criteria as in a checklist or a more detailed rubric. For example, in the program review process, analysis of documents is used to provide historical context and to assess the progression and implementation of a program. Document analysis complements other assessment methods and is seldom used alone.

Tests or Quizzes. Tests or quizzes are used to assess what students have learned as a result of participating in a program or service. These need to be aligned with a program's content and delivery. Students are presented with quantitative or qualitative questions where they must report what they have learned. For example, a quantitative question would require students to pick the correct response from a short list of possible answers. A qualitative question might be a fill-in-the-blank, short answer, or essay question. Tests or quizzes can be implemented pre- and postexperience to ascertain gains in learning or used solely at the end of an experience to assess learning. Student performance on national exams and placement exams can also be used in this type of assessment.

Rubrics. Staff can use rubrics to collect both quantitative and qualitative direct evidence of student learning. A rubric includes a set of criteria and a scale for scoring and is used to assess a student's performance, project, or paper. There are different types of rubrics ranging from a checklist (*student meets or does not meet a criterion*) to three- to five-point scales that measure the level of attainment along the different dimensions of the activity. For example, a three-point scale might include *does not meet standard, meets standard,* or *exceeds standard,* and describe the criteria by which each standard is defined. Rubrics typically include a place for reviewer comments about why a score was given for each criterion. Rubrics are used to evaluate works such as capstone projects, performances, portfolios, work samples, internal or external juried reviews of projects, written compositions, and music and photo analysis submissions. Rubrics can be both a direct and indirect method of collecting assessment evidence and are further addressed in the next section.

Indirect Evidence

Surveys. A survey is essentially a set of questions staff use to measure viewpoints such as student satisfaction, preparedness, perceived benefits of an event, plans after graduation, or perceived worth of education and degree, to name a few. Surveys created in-house are developed around intended outcomes of an experience. Surveys from an external source need to match goals and intended outcomes of a program. Most survey questions include a response scale measuring the degree of a perception (e.g., Likert scales to measure students' levels of agreement). A scaled response question can be followed with a qualitative prompt to probe why a particular rating was given. Surveys administered after an intervention or event typically measure the student's experience of that event and perhaps ask for a perception of the learning that resulted. Surveys are also used to gauge external stakeholders' views of students' skills and abilities. Stakeholders can include potential and current employers of students who want to assess student preparedness for the workforce or supervisors of students participating in internships, practica, and service-learning experiences who want to gauge student progress.

Another category of surveys referred to as benchmark studies provides comparative data with other similar institutions (e.g., National Survey of Student Engagement [NSSE], National College Health Assessment [NCHA], and College Learning Assessment [CLA]). Benchmark studies allow an institution to compare its students to other students, both internal and external to the university and often at the same grade level, and provide trend data to track changes in students over time.

Interviews. Interviews can also be an indirect assessment depending on the types of questions asked of students. If students are asked to share their educational experiences or to reflect on their learning, as in student exit interviews, then this is an indirect assessment. Although this type of indirect data provides valuable information, it is recommended that if making programming decisions other assessment evidence be collected in conjunction with this method.

Rubrics. Previously explained as a direct method, there are also ways in which rubrics are effective as indirect methods. The determination of whether a rubric is a direct or indirect method will ultimately rely on what question the student affairs professional wants answered. In this case, self-scored rubrics allow students to evaluate their perceptions of gains in learning new material or in the quality of their own work, such as submissions of student portfolios, projects, performances, or papers. An example of a combination of indirect and direct assessment would be to have the staff member and student use the same rubric to evaluate the student's work. The conversation that ensues will facilitate the student's learning and point to opportunities for growth. Indirectly, having students provide feedback about the quality of their work allows educators to assess the extent to which students have gauged vital concepts such as self-efficacy or accurate impressions of self.

Journals. Journaling allows the student to reflect on his or her own learning and experiences. Often a prompt is provided to guide students in their writing. Although these student journals are often private, staff can use the same prompts but request open answers to develop other assessment methods. For example, staff could use these prompts and have students write a short essay about their experiences as part of an alternative spring break experience. Some student affairs professionals have incorporated social media into this method by asking students to author blogs during their alternative break experience.

Other Data Sources. There are other data sources available to track student engagement, retention, and persistence. These include participation rates, document analysis, and data from external stakeholders (unpaid internship supervisors, agency supervisors in service-learning placements, job placement statistics, and secondary analysis of documents/data from another source).

University metrics are most often used to measure student retention and persistence, but they do not provide direct evidence for student learning outcomes. For example, universities often report student data regarding entry such as GPA, preadmission test scores, and high school ranking. Once matriculated, data might include student–faculty ratio and student credit hours. After students have graduated, universities often consider GPA, overall retention rates, fall-to-fall retention, four- to six-year graduation rates, the number of students employed, and average starting salary (Schuh & Upcraft, 2001).

National comparative data such as those provided by the National Center for Education Statistics help place an institution in relation to other similar institutions. In addition, there are reports of university ratings and rankings, such as the U.S. News College Compass reports or the Carnegie Civic Engagement Classification, that may be useful.

Accurate and Comprehensive Data

Regardless of assessment method used, it is essential that staff consider, as much as possible, whether the assessment method will yield data that are rigorous (accurate and comprehensive). The data need to accurately reflect—in detail—what occurred. Rigor requires sound processes in place throughout the assessment cycle that allow one to trust the results generated from assessment. The process of determining rigor applies to both quantitative and qualitative methods.

Quantitative Rigor

Assessing accuracy and comprehensiveness with quantitative data is very straightforward but is not the same as psychometrically examining reliability and validity, which can be a bit more rigorous. As this is not a chapter on measurement theory, let us look at this from a practitioner's perspective and what strategies student affairs professionals, who are often not statisticians, might employ for developing rigor-grounded approaches.

Ensuring Alignment. It is imperative that the program goals, activities, and assessments align with each other if one is to trust the interpretation of findings. Start with the end in mind. What do staff hope students will know at the end of their program or service? Working backward, what activities will occur to allow this to happen?

Defining Constructs. Once staff have determined what students will learn as a result of participation, they must then decide what specifically to measure. For example, for a student leadership program, in what aspects of leadership will students demonstrate proficiency? These aspects will then serve as the constructs to measure during assessment. The constructs need to be well defined. One way to do so is to define them based on relevant research, theory, and standards. For example, in our development of an employee self-evaluation scale we began the process by first identifying the construct(s)/aspect(s) of employee performance to measure (Wise & Hatfield, 2014). We used *Professional Competency Areas for Student Affairs Practitioners* (American College Personnel Association & National Association of Student Personnel Administrators, 2010) and our human resource guidelines to develop our scale.

Pilot Testing and Reviewing. All assessments need to be reviewed by others who have some level of expertise developing instruments and protocols as well as with the student affairs functions in question. I recommend including staff and potential respondents in this process. The review process should ask the following questions: (a) Do the items appear to measure the construct(s) of interest? (b) Are students asked to respond in a way that makes sense to the questions(s) being asked? (c) Are the items unambiguous and free of harmful or biased language? It is imperative for the assessment method to yield data that are credible but also address program goals.

Qualitative Rigor

In analyzing the rigor of qualitative data, it is essential that the conclusions drawn from the patterns/themes that have emerged from the data be confirmed or verified to ensure they accurately reflect participants' views of reality (Berg, 2001). Staff need to verify that findings are accurate from the standpoint of the researcher, the participants, or the readers of an account. Creswell (1998) provides some very straightforward ways to verify accuracy:

- *Triangulating data.* This process means using multiple data sources, methods, and evidence to form themes or categories and to corroborate findings. For example, if staff use a survey to explore students' perception of a new policy, a follow-up focus group would elucidate survey findings as well as open the door to perceptions that might run counter to findings. Having a more complete picture provides more credibility.
- *Using member checks.* In this process, staff interpretations of qualitative data are shared with participants to determine the accuracy of descriptions, interpretations, and findings. Any discrepancies between staff and participant perspectives are discussed and changes to interpretations made.
- *Providing rich, detailed, contextual description.* In presenting findings, staff provide detailed descriptions of the setting, participants, processes, and interactions that will place the results in context.
- *Clarifying researcher stance.* All research has biases; the more open to interpretation data are, the more likely that biases will have an influence. For example, a staff member who is evaluating her own program through qualitative methods brings assumptions, beliefs, and biases to the process. This staff member could acknowledge biases at the outset and remove herself from data collection and interpretation, or she could acknowledge her stance in the analysis and interpretation of findings. In the second scenario, she would rely on feedback from participants and a person external to the study to ensure processes and findings are as representative as possible.
- *Providing counter information.* Qualitative data are analyzed with an eye to seeking out information that might run counter to beliefs, assumptions, or derived themes. For example, if a program is based

on theory, it would be easy then to look for evidence that supports the theory. It is also important to look for information that runs counter to theory.

- *Collaborating with others.* A person external to data collection and interpretation examines the processes (research steps, decisions, activities) and products (narrative accounts, conclusions) to determine their accuracy. Participants can also be included in the review of interpretations and findings to determine accuracy.

- *Generalizing findings.* Providing rich, detailed, contextualized description helps place the reader in the context and allows the reader to determine if findings are transferable to another setting. In addition, collecting data in which multiple informants and multiple data-collection methods are used can strengthen the study's usefulness for other settings.

Rigor for Both Quantitative and Qualitative Methods

Regardless of whether quantitative or qualitative methods are used, it is important to include students in the whole assessment process and use their formative feedback to help improve programs and services. For example, in clarifying mission, vision, and values, staff can solicit student feedback through focus groups, individual interviews, and participation in meetings. Moreover, in the creation of assessment instruments, sample a subset of the target student population to review the instruments and to determine if they actually measure what is intended and that the instructions on completing the assessment and actual questions/tasks are clear, specific, and understandable. Also, include students in the interpretation of assessment findings and the development of recommendations for their use. By including student feedback in all phases of the assessment process, staff are more likely to find that students are engaged because they know their voices matter and they have been heard.

Good assessment plans incorporate ways to give students feedback about how the data are used and what changes have resulted from their responses. Examples include posting results on program websites, in school newspapers, on social media sites, in flyers, and in newsletters; projecting assessment results prior to a movie; or presenting results at a student event.

Conclusion

This chapter provides a guide for robust assessment so that your division will gather evidence that meets your institutional mission, vision, and goals.

As a result, your staff should now be prepared to best select the appropriate tools to measure their impact on the student experience and you will be able to trust that the data collected are accurate and comprehensive. Data not shared, though, serve no benefit. SSAOs must expect their units to share data and to tell their stories of their collective impact on students; moreover, sharing needs to occur both internal and external to the university. In the next chapter, Christakis and Demeter provide examples of divisions of student affairs who have done well with telling their story to and sharing assessment data with diverse stakeholders.

References

American College Personnel Association & National Association of Student Personnel Administrators. (2010). *ACPA/NASPA professional competency areas for student affairs practitioners.* Retrieved from www.naspa.org/programs/profdev/

Berg, B. L. (2001). *Qualitative research methods for the social sciences* (4th ed.). Boston, MA: Allyn & Bacon.

Creswell, J. W. (1998). *Qualitative inquiry and research design: Choosing among five traditions.* Thousand Oaks, CA: Sage.

Culp, M. (2012). Starting the culture of evidence journey. In M. M. Culp & G. J. Dungy (Eds.), *Building a culture of evidence in student affairs: A guide for leaders and practitioners* (p. 1). Washington, DC: NASPA.

Schuh, J. H., & Upcraft, M. L. (2001). *Assessment practice in student affairs: An applications manual.* San Francisco, CA: Jossey-Bass.

Student Affairs Leadership Council. (2009). *The data-driven student affairs enterprise: Strategies and best practices for instilling a culture of accountability.* Washington, DC: The Advisory Board Company.

Wise, V. L., & Barham, M. A. (2012). Assessment matters: Moving beyond surveys. *About Campus, 17*(2), 26–29.

Wise, V. L., & Hatfield, L. J. (2014, Summer). Employee evaluation using professional competencies. *Developments, 12*(2). Retrieved from http://www.myacpa.org/publications/developments/volume-12-issue-2

10

TENET TEN: DISSEMINATE DATA TO LEVERAGE BUY-IN AND PROMOTE UTILITY TO THE CAMPUS COMMUNITY

Michael N. Christakis and Marylee Demeter

SSAO's Perspective

Christine A. Bouchard

Seven years ago, when the University at Albany's student affairs division (known as Student Success at the time, it is now referred to as Student Affairs) launched its first serious venture into the world of assessment, we did not completely comprehend all it would take to establish a truly effective assessment plan. We happily embarked on a thoughtful collection of data across the many departments within Student Affairs, but soon found ourselves buried in facts without enough time built into our process to make sense of it all and with no clear approach on how to best utilize material we had gathered. We were data rich but information poor.

This tenet espouses the importance of collecting data that have real utility and of moving beyond data collection to interpreting and sharing the data—both within and across the units of the division. The premise guiding this chapter is that we collect information that champions our desired story, and we tell that story in diverse ways to our various and varied audiences. The goal is to translate data into information that creates a picture of our students, articulates the information to key constituents, and allows us to better demonstrate not only what we do well, but also where we can do better. We had numerous starts and stops in our assessment journey at the University at Albany, but we know now that how we tell the story is a vital consideration in our assessment processes.

Data Rich, Information Poor

Student affairs professionals are surrounded by data: institutional data, survey data, facilities usage, and student participation in activities are just some examples. Most of us think we are engaging in effective assessment practices because we collect these data, but that is only half the battle. To truly engage in assessment that informs our key stakeholders and decision makers, we need to go beyond gathering and providing data; we need to share *information.*

One challenge to overcome is our use of the terms *data* and *information* interchangeably, as though one was synonymous with the other. For our purposes, *data* are "factual information (as measurements or statistics) used as a basis for reasoning, discussion, or calculation" ("Data," *Merriam-Webster Online Dictionary,* n.d.), whereas *information* is defined in several ways, most notably as "the communication or reception of knowledge or intelligence," "knowledge obtained from investigation, study, or instruction," or "a signal or character (as in a communication system or computer) representing data" ("Information," *Merriam-Webster Online Dictionary,* n.d.). *Data* are what we "process"; *information* is our output. The apparent breakdown that occurs when we confuse the two terms stifles assessment efforts and frustrates assessment professionals. Because we view data and information as interchangeable, we fail to process our data and develop an accurate representation to convey necessary information needed in our decision-making processes.

As student affairs professionals, providing access to data is not enough to inform our stakeholders and decision makers. In its raw form, data are unstructured and disorganized. Those interested in the information usually do not have the time to organize it, and they likely do not possess the tools or knowledge to provide the necessary structure for interpretation. As assessment professionals, we must provide a service: transforming raw data into organized, structured information that can easily be understood and used by others to make decisions about programs and services. This is our job but the senior student affairs officer (SSAO) can have an important role in telling that story.

When we move beyond gathering to processing data, the information needs to be promoted and shared among individuals in an easily comprehensible form, resulting in several benefits for consumers of said information. The consistent use of findings—in the form of evidentiary data turned into information—helps inform decisions and sends an important message that stakeholders' voices matter and that we are responding to their concerns. This in turn allows our stakeholders—most important among them, our students—to develop trust and willingness to help the institution improve our programs and services. Furthermore, it motivates these same stakeholders to participate in future assessment activities because they see that their opinions and experiences matter. Often, the assessment coordinator or team leader may take on this responsibility; however, when the SSAO has the opportunity to interact with stakeholders she or he can expand on the story we are telling. She or he can interpret the story in a way that makes sense for the person with whom the SSAO interacts: the institution's president, parents of students, donors, and other student affairs staff, for example.

Sharing results also promotes greater accountability and transparency in the decision-making process by illustrating the reasoning behind decisions and actions. Providing such evidence is proof positive that we are not creating or cutting programs on a whim, or spending money on services we *think* will work. Rather, it shows we are serious about student success and will use relevant information to ensure our students are achieving learning outcomes as a result of our programs and services.

This chapter approaches information sharing from both the perspective of the SSAO as "chief assessment spokesperson" and that of a student affairs assessment professional in providing the SSAO and other key stakeholders with pertinent information. We detail eight essential elements for effective information-sharing and highlight some select best practices.

SSAO as Chief Assessment Spokesperson

Every SSAO must demonstrate leadership through serving as a chief advocate, ally, champion, and spokesperson for sound assessment practice. SSAOs who have bought into the value of assessment understand the power of good data and sound information. There is no better spokesperson for a student affairs division's assessment findings than the SSAO. Furthermore, there is no one better to view the organization strategically and tactically and determine how data can be used to enhance programs and services to stakeholders than the SSAO. Whether at a meeting with the campus president, at the table with other SSAOs, or in interactions with trustees, students, faculty, or alumni, an assessment-savvy, data-driven SSAO is far and away the single greatest spokesperson for a division's assessment findings.

What better way to add value to a division's programs and services than to hear one of your SSAOs give stakeholders his or her "stump speech" laden with facts, figures, and findings, as evidence of how data has shaped the division's priorities?

Information-Sharing: Making Findings Resonate With Stakeholders

Having an assessment champion and spokesperson is an important start to sharing our results, but how do we make our findings resonate with stakeholders? Consider this: When was the last time you actually sat down and read that 10-page executive summary? Two related challenges arise when trying to make assessment findings as user friendly as possible. First, the sheer amount of information we are trying to share is often far in excess of what a normal person can consume in one sitting, let alone on the run or in between meetings, as our students and campus presidents are often found. Boiling down the data from a 150-question survey, analyzing a 30-page focus group transcript, or coding 400+ open-ended responses are not processes for the assessment faint of heart. Of the 150 questions, which responses were most interesting (dare we say "surprising")? While coding the focus group transcript of the open-ended questions, what themes emerged as the most frequent (or even alarming)? In much the same way that raw data do not easily become information, information is not easily translated to stakeholders through that 10-page executive summary of last spring's survey of resident students. Whereas the first challenge for the student affairs professional is making information manageable, the second challenge is making that same information interesting. No one wants to read 10 pages of text. Their eyes will likely glaze over halfway through the third page. Developing interesting and innovative ways to present findings, particularly given competing interests on the part of various stakeholders, is arguably as daunting a challenge as making those findings manageable.

When it is time to communicate our information, the best strategy is to use visual representations. A visual approach enables decision makers to quickly view results without having to muddle through jargon. It makes findings comprehensible, regardless of a stakeholder's knowledge of a particular topic or issue. Stakeholders are hungry for information and even hungrier for user-friendly and transparent representations that ensure our message is getting across. Information graphics, or "infographics," are graphic visual representations of data or information intended to present otherwise complex information quickly and clearly (Byrne & Cook, 2013). For our purposes, *infographics* are defined as any graphic representation of data or information for purposes of making findings comprehensible to key stakeholders. Infographics are versatile, in that they can be incorporated into newsletters, websites, and various forms of social media. They are easily shared among university partners, which help disseminate our results to a large audience in a meaningful way. A single infographic (e.g., Figures 10.1 and 10.2) can communicate complex results from our assessment efforts in a way that is easy to understand and use in the decision-making process.

Figure 10.1   Infographic: Sharing Assessment Data About Student Experiences at The University of Albany

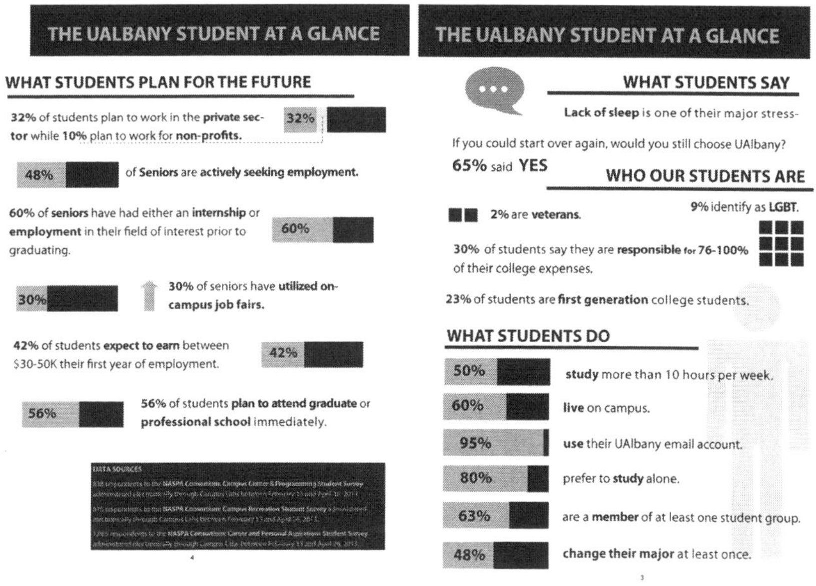

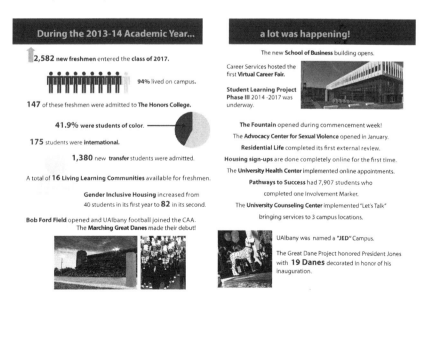

Figure 10.2   Infographic: Sharing "The Year in Review" Assessment Data at The University of Albany

Eight Essential Elements for Effective Information-Sharing

Empowering yourself or your SSAO with authentic, powerful, user-friendly, and actionable information is an important step in ensuring that your data-collecting efforts do not go unheralded and furthering the division's assessment agenda as a powerful tool in enhancing programs, services, and activities on campus. We detail here eight essential elements for effective information-sharing.

Element 1: Authenticity

For our purposes, authenticity reflects both the reliability and validity of a particular assessment and its associated findings. In assessment, we frame *reliability* as the degree to which an instrument produces consistent results and the instrument's *validity* as the extent to which it measures what it is purported to measure (Palomba & Banta, 1999). The information the SSAO articulates must be absolutely, unquestionably authentic. Anything short of this threshold exposes the SSAO and the division to criticism. We cannot emphasize enough the importance of information based on reliable, valid data sources. In much the same way you would not intentionally provide your SSAO with misleading information, you certainly would not promote bunk information either. The slightest bit of uncertainty regarding a fact or figure should give you pause. It only takes one disingenuous data point to undo a stakeholder's confidence in the information your office is providing.

Element 2: Know Your Audience

You must establish early on who exactly your primary audience is. The most common mistake is to treat the audience as anyone. If data are based on visitors to the university health center, you probably should not post it in your career development center and vice versa. If you are seeking to engage first-year students in cocurricular activities, a blast e-mail to all students espousing the benefits of being involved probably will not be as effective as a targeted campaign in first-year students' residence areas.

Element 3: Present User-Friendly Information

The SSAO should not be put in a position of struggling to clarify what a particular piece of information means. The facts and figures should speak for themselves. The fact that the SSAO is articulating said findings only emphasizes the relative importance of the information at hand. The information and the authority of the SSAO should reinforce each other. Putting authentic, powerful, and user-friendly information in the hands of a knowledgeable SSAO should be a value-added proposition. To drive this item home further, your audience should not be expected to have to decipher the information you have provided. Rather, you should be providing clearly articulated, easy-to-understand information. Even though your information may be authentic, if your audience cannot fully comprehend what you are trying to articulate, they likely will not give you a second chance at a first impression.

Element 4: Use High-Quality Visuals

We have emphasized the use of infographics, but we cannot overemphasize that the most successful campaigns use high-quality visuals. It is quicker and easier to understand a thoughtful, clear image than to stop and read lines of text, regardless of how little text there may be. Further, high-quality visuals have the added benefit of drawing your audience in, making them stop and notice.

Element 5: Choose Your Outlets Wisely

We began to address this in element 2; in much the same way that you should know your audience, you should also know how to get to your audience. We will not debate the pros and cons of e-mail, social media, poster campaigns, and the like—that is up to you and your specific campus climate. Only you know how your campus and the various audiences and stakeholders will react across various outlets. Identifying the specific outlets that are most effective may take some trial and error and even after you have established what might be considered good, reliable outlets, stakeholders (students) change and the way we get information to them should change in turn.

Element 6: Do Not Become "Stale"; Nobody Likes "Old News"

A poster detailing data from 2006 just is not as impactful as a poster detailing data that were gathered earlier in the semester. The same is true for out-of-date websites or social media pages and old annual reports sitting in waiting rooms. If there are new data, there should be new information. Staying up to date makes stakeholders want more (or so we would like to think). But in much the same way that disingenuous information pushes your audience away, so too does infrequent and stale information. Be strategic about when you introduce new information, how you introduce it, and how long it stays in the public domain. There is no harm in archiving data, but there is harm in featuring old data. If SSAOs are armed with information that reflects the past or present condition of their students' experiences, they should also come prepared to articulate how they plan to effect change in their students' experiences accordingly (for the better).

Element 7: Make Information Actionable

We have detailed why we share data. Among those reasons is building trust with your stakeholders. The information the SSAO is sharing needs to have a compelling, powerful, and actionable narrative associated with it. There is no exact formula for what constitutes a powerful message, however. Residence hall occupancy rates, for instance, that have remained constant over the past five years may not seem powerful enough for the SSAO to use unless the division had hoped that the university would have experienced an increase during that same period. Understanding the tenor and tone of various campus-based issues will assist the assessment professional in providing the SSAO with the information necessary to make a powerful statement supported by authentic data. By making the information you are sharing actionable—that is, something tangible that the reader can see or do—it engages the audience in a deeper, more meaningful way. Directing them to visit an office, a website, an event, a program, or an activity also ensures a level of information recall on the part of the reader. Utilizing quick response (QR) codes or articulating instructive statements are powerful ways of engaging your audience after they have read or heard the information.

Element 8: Appreciate the Importance of Following Up

Ultimately, sharing information based on assessment findings is an exercise in "closing the loop." As previously stated, collecting data for the sake of collecting data is an exercise in futility and a big waste of everyone's time. Appreciating the importance of following up with stakeholders who have provided you with the data and/or have a role in effecting change based on findings is an important foundational element for sharing information.

In the next section we provide examples of how these essential elements have been realized through some outstanding assessment practices in modern-day student affairs work. These examples will provide opportunities for the application of the lessons thus far in the chapter.

Best Practices: Delivering Data, Informing Stakeholders

This section provides examples of marketing efforts that illustrate the eight essential elements, most saliently the importance of following up. What these institutions have in common is a focus on the importance of student opinions in developing and improving programs and services, coupled with a commitment to using state-of-the-art practices in communicating assessment efforts and results. For further information on these specific efforts, as well as the sources for quoted material in the following sections, see the websites listed at the end of the chapter under "Online Resources."

At the University of Georgia, the Division for Student Affairs' Your Voice Has Been Heard campaign was "derived from the belief that students' voices are a valuable part of the decisions student affairs makes regarding the programs and services it offers to students." Throughout the year, the division identifies and communicates examples of how information collected from students has been used to enhance their educational experience. Similarly, the University of North Carolina at Wilmington developed the We've Heard Your Voice campaign (Figure 10.3) in an effort to "communicate assessment results and changes made in our programs and services at UNCW based on [assessment] findings. These changes demonstrate that the time students spend taking surveys really makes a difference."

The University at Albany's (UAlbany) Division of Student Affairs introduced the Your Voice campaign to promote awareness of assessment initiatives and findings to its students. At UAlbany, "Student Affairs values students' input during the assessment process and utilizes their insights regularly and [the campaign] communicates the outcomes of Student Affairs assessments and informs the UAlbany community as to the importance of assessment and research findings."

The *Penn State Pulse* is an online survey initiative developed in the spring of 1995 by the Division of Student Affairs at Penn State University to gather feedback on student issues, expectations, usage, and satisfaction in order to get a better understanding of students' opinions on a wide-ranging list of subjects. *Pulse* surveys are reviewed and approved by the Pennsylvania State

Figure 10.3 Communicating Assessment: We've Heard Your Voice at the University of North Carolina at Wilmington

University Office for Research Protections and require participant consent. High participation rates, large respondent numbers, and verification that the demographics of respondents are consistent with the population suggest that the survey results are generally representative of the student body. Results are reported in summary form and are available approximately one month after a survey is completed. Results are posted online and shared with university administrators, staff, faculty, and students. Notice of new results is sent via the Student Affairs Research and Assessment listserv, which anyone can opt to receive (simply send an e-mail to saraoffice@psu.edu).

UAlbany's *The Pulse of Student Success* is a publication that details recent assessment findings based on research conducted by UAlbany's Division of Student Affairs. In an easy-to-read format, the *Pulse* (Figure 10.4) informs and educates the UAlbany community about the continued assessment and research efforts of Student Affairs to create an environment within which all community members can engage, learn, and succeed.

Briefing Books and Annual Reports

Briefing books and annual reports remain an effective vehicle for disseminating information. The key to success is employing effective marketing strategies for sharing and promoting these materials. In preparing these publications, it is important to capitalize on the value of visual representations and effective technologies to disseminate the information efficiently and effectively to a wide audience, as illustrated by elements 2, 4, and 5. It is also important to promote their value as reference materials for future assessment endeavors, thus making the information actionable.

Rutgers, The State University of New Jersey, and UAlbany each publish an *Annual Briefing Book* online each summer, providing a snapshot of individual student affairs unit activities, including points of pride and strategic goals for the coming year. The publications also showcase strategic plans and learning goals; provide visual representations of results to illustrate progress toward unit goals; and highlight collaborations within, across, and beyond the division of student affairs. UAlbany, in particular, capitalizes on the use of infographics, illustrating the element of high-quality visuals. Additional examples of student affairs reports and briefing books include the Stony Brook University Division of Student Affairs *Briefing Book,* the Alfred University *Briefing Book,* the University of Alabama student affairs *Annual Report,* the Iowa State *Annual Report,* and the University of Nebraska at Omaha *Annual Report.*

Public dissemination of such briefing books and annual reports provides essential information for stakeholders, particularly parents of current and prospective students investing in their child's education. Easy online access also provides state and federal funding agencies the necessary information

Figure 10.4 Communicating Assessment: Sharing Results From the Pulse of Student Success at the University of Albany

when making decisions in supporting initiatives in regard to student affairs programming and services. The information provided is also used to inform new and continuing assessment projects throughout the division. Review of the previous years' activities helps to identify and employ effective strategies as well as note what did not work very well to improve processes for the next assessment, making the information actionable. Overall, briefing books and annual reports foster transparency and can be used as a model for developing materials as you build a culture of assessment on your campus.

Briefing books and annual reports can be cheaply and easily disseminated when published in PDF format and made available online using a variety of innovative publishing technologies. Several institutions publish their reports on issuu.com, an online publications repository featuring search functioning and categorical groupings. Alternatively, institutions may house reports and briefing books on file-sharing sites such as Dropbox.com, allowing users to create direct links to reports that can be embedded as a link on divisional websites or sent privately through e-mail, particularly to donors who make monetary contributions specifically to student affairs.

Conclusion

Student affairs professionals are often surrounded by data but fall short in effectively translating those data into information. It is our responsibility to act on this evidence, because sharing our results demonstrates the value of our programs and services in supporting student development. Promoting our results also helps increase transparency and accountability, as we can directly show stakeholders our programs are achieving what we set out to achieve, thus limiting skepticism and doubt in our financial investments.

Stakeholders become empowered through data and information gleaned from assessment activities within student affairs. Assessment results enable SSAOs to develop programs and services that students want, leading to increased student engagement and involvement on campus. Students see that the time and effort they put into providing feedback are not in vain; we directly show them how the feedback they provide leads to changes on campus that matter to them. This not only increases the chances they will participate in programs and utilize services, but also feeds into the development of a campus-wide culture of evidence among our students, increasing the likelihood they will take the time to participate in future assessment endeavors.

Marketing our results also advances the role of student affairs professionals as educators, with an emphasis on cocurricular experiences. When we connect learning outcomes directly to programs and services and share evidence of student learning gathered through assessment efforts, we strengthen our role as teachers and mentors, demonstrating the value of both the program/service and the individuals involved in their delivery. In an age where we see increased demands for accountability and decreased opportunities for funding, sharing our results strengthens the trust our stakeholders have in our programs and services, as well as improves our ability to enhance student learning through involvement outside the classroom. Demonstrating our role in student learning thus helps dispel myths about administrators in higher education, particularly when institutions are increasingly criticized for allocating resources to administrators. Showing our stakeholders our direct involvement in student learning can help justify the need for student affairs administration and our impact on student success.

Marketing information gathered through our assessment practices also strengthens ties to our counterparts in academic affairs, as illustrating our results encourages shared learning goals between both sides of the house. Transparency of assessment efforts enables us to show how our programs contribute to institution-wide learning goals, while dispelling the perception of student affairs as providing unnecessary "amenities." Continued marketing efforts ultimately help break down the misconception of the role of student affairs as simply providing "fun"; rather, we help construct the impression of student affairs as a partner in student success, while demonstrating our commitment to institutional collaboration.

Our marketing efforts also help foster partnerships with various members of the wider community. Marketing results helps parents feel at ease when we provide evidence that shows our role in helping their children develop and grow into self-regulated, knowledgeable adults ready for entry into the workforce. This in turn strengthens the likelihood they will continue to support their children in persisting at our institution. Our results benefit the parents of prospective students as well, as the information empowers them in the decision-making process of helping their children decide where to attend college.

Finally, sharing our findings allows us to lead by example, empowering student affairs professionals to develop sound assessment programs, including strategies for marketing results. When we champion our efforts, we show others that assessment matters and that it is worth the time and effort we put into it. It also shows assessment doesn't have to be a dreaded activity focused solely on evaluation; when we show how assessment improves decision making, it puts others at ease because they know the data are not used to judge individuals. Rather, the results are used to make a positive difference in the lives of our students and tell the story of how student affairs contributes to the goals of modern-day higher education.

Online Resources

Alfred University, *Briefing Book*
aura.alfred.edu/bitstream/handle/10829/4988/AU%20Briefing%20
Book%202013-14%20pdf%20copy%20for%20Kathy.pdf?sequence=1

Department of Student Affairs Assessment at the University of Georgia, Your
Voice Has Been Heard campaign
studentaffairs.uga.edu/assess/yourvoice/index.htm

Dropbox
www.dropbox.com

Iowa State, *Annual Report*
http://www.studentaffairs.iastate.edu/whatwedo/forms/sa_annual_report_11-12.pdf

Issuu
issuu.com/signin?onLogin=http%3A%2F%2Fissuu.com%2Fhome#/signin

Penn State, *Pulse* Program.
studentaffairs.psu.edu/assessment/pulse/
studentaffairs.psu.edu/assessment/chronopulse.shtml

Rutgers, The State University of New Jersey, Division of Student Affairs *Annual Report, 2011–2012*
irp.rutgers.edu/MSA-PRR-2013/Documents/SA%20Annual%20Report%202011-2012.pdf

Stony Brook University Division of Student Affairs, *Briefing Book*
studentaffairs.stonybrook.edu/stu/briefingbook/briefing_book_2012-13.pdf

University at Albany, *Annual Briefing Book*
www.albany.edu/studentsuccess/assessment/BriefingBook/Briefing%20Book%202012-13.pdf

University at Albany, Division of Student Affairs, Your Voice campaign
www.albany.edu/studentsuccess/assessment/your_voice.shtml

University at Albany, *The Pulse of Student Success*
www.albany.edu/studentsuccess/assessment/pulse.shtml

University of Alabama Student Affairs, *Annual Report*
issuu.com/uastudentaffairs/docs/annualreport_2013

University of Nebraska at Omaha, *Briefing Book*
issuu.com/unodsa/docs/unostudentaffairsannualreport2013

University of North Carolina at Wilmington, We've Heard Your Voice campaign
uncw.edu/studentaffairs/assessment

References

Byrne, D., & Cook, G. (2013). *The best American infographics 2013*. Boston, MA: Houghton Mifflin Harcourt.

Data. (n.d.). In *Merriam-Webster' Online Dictionary*. Retrieved from http://www.merriam-webster.com/dictionary/data

Information. (n.d.). In *Merriam-Webster's Online Dictionary.* Retrieved from http:// www.merriam-webster.com/dictionary/information

Palomba, C. A., & Banta, T. W. (1999). *Assessment essentials: Planning, implementing, and improving assessment in higher education* (Higher and Adult Education Series). San Francisco, CA: Jossey-Bass.

EPILOGUE: USING THE TEN TENETS TO NAVIGATE CHANGE

Amber Garrison Duncan and Kevin Kruger

Understanding the nature of current changes in higher education is critical as we look ahead to how student affairs practices may need to adapt. Divisions that have already gone through the work to establish and sustain a culture of assessment will have prepared themselves well to respond to change. Although these challenges will affect the entire field of student affairs, the best way to be prepared to lead as a senior student affairs officer (SSAO) on campus is to create a culture of assessment, one that is comfortable with questions and uses evidence to make the best decisions to increase student success.

The purpose of this chapter is to provide a brief overview of six higher education reforms taking place that will influence student affairs and our assessment priorities. The issues explored here include the following:

1. Emphasis on institutions being student centered and learning based
2. New frameworks that define the common learning outcomes associated with degrees and other credentials
3. Direct assessment of curricular and cocurricular learning
4. Extended transcripts
5. Use of big data analytics to shape practices and demonstrate effectiveness
6. Accountability methods tied to student outcome measures

This list of reforms is not meant to be exhaustive; rather, it is meant to provide an overview of the major initiatives that are likely to influence the role of student affairs assessment leaders in shaping responses to the challenges and opportunities ahead. Once each of the six reforms is explored, direct connections are made for student affairs assessment by Kevin Kruger, president of NASPA. In closing, a call to action is issued for senior leaders to commit to thinking through the implications of these reforms and using evidence to create new models and practices in student affairs.

Student Centered, Learning Based

Pressure has been mounting for institutions to be held accountable for *student outcomes*, defined as maximizing both the number of students who finish degrees and the quality of learning behind those degrees. As critiques of the academy have grown more sophisticated, focusing on degree completion and student learning, so too have the emerging policies that are now bearing down on institutions. The good news is that, overall, these reforms are focused on making institutions student centered and learning based, meaning students are prioritized in a system where learning is the measure of success.

As higher education responds, new definitions of *quality* and *learning* are materializing, measurement of student completion is becoming more mainstream, and redefined best practices are emerging. Given these fundamental shifts, student affairs will need to explore different ways to function on campus, and assessment will become a major driver to position student affairs as contributory, meaningful, and relevant to higher education.

What assessment can do in a student-centered, learning-based environment is sharpen focus on the experiences that best meet student learning needs. Because students are at the center, learning experiences should be created around them that best deliver on the outcomes associated with their credentials. This means putting students ahead of preconceived notions of who does what as well as crossing traditional silos. For instance, many campuses are creating more generalist approaches to their work by combining housing and financial aid outcomes or academic advising and student organization advising. Again, this reinforces the fact that learning and support need to be structured around the student. Another way assessment can serve the field is by identifying where programs or services are not contributing to student success so that a "stop doing" list can be created that frees up resources to be directed to those practices that make the most difference for students.

Defining Quality of Credentials

Although previous measures of accountability focused primarily on student outcomes related to completing college, the focus is shifting to the concerns of future employers, who may seek answers about the value of what students have learned or clarity about what college graduates should be expected to know and do—or even whether a college degree is valuable in itself.

Associations representing higher education have responded and are taking the lead in an effort to create a shared understanding of the learning outcomes associated with a college degree. For instance, in 2005 the Association of American Colleges and Universities (AAC&U) launched the Essential Learning Outcomes initiative as a benchmark to define the learning that should be represented in a liberal college education. Most often these outcomes are present in general education. The broad outcome areas are knowledge of human cultures and the physical and natural world, intellectual and practical skills, personal and social responsibility, and integrative and applied learning. Each outcome has more specific measures associated with it, so colleges can integrate these goals in the curriculum and cocurriculum as well as measure student learning accordingly.

Expanding on the Essential Learning Outcomes, as of 2011, the Degree Qualifications Profile (DQP) has emerged as the framework in the United States defining the learning outcomes for associate's, bachelor's, and master's degrees, regardless of major. The DQP was developed from the field as faculty provided feedback about the outcomes most important to degrees. Institutions can now use the DQP to align courses and cocurricular learning experiences in order to achieve the quality of learning described. With more than 500 institutions now using the DQP as a way to meet quality expectations and accreditors mentioning the DQP as a way to assess quality for accreditation, *accountability for quality learning* has been definitively and conclusively defined by higher education and employers. This marks an important partnership as faculty and employers are best positioned to define what *high quality* means for both lifelong learning and employability. This partnership is being called upon to stretch even further so the competencies associated with all credentials (degrees, certificates, certifications, nondegree credentials) in the United States are defined through the beta version of the Connecting Credentials Framework initiative launched in June 2015. This framework will create a common language and description for the vast array of credentials so that recipients will understand what they should be able to know and do as a result of the credential they have earned.

Student affairs professionals must be familiar with the characteristics of high-quality learning in order to intentionally incorporate and then assess these approaches in appropriate programs, services, and interventions. This is important to ensure not only that student affairs is considered an equal partner in student learning, but also that the learning we value contributes to positive, marketable degree outcomes for students. Divisions should come to a common understanding of the outcomes provided across the cocurriculum. This suggests that the concept of a curriculum map, or a student affairs cocurriculum map, could be of use in understanding where intentional programming across the division provides learning that is mapped to degree outcomes.

Competency-Based Education

With accountability measures for completion and quality being mapped to and associated with specific outcomes, competency-based education (CBE) is becoming a more common way to structure student learning. CBE is a flexible model for students to earn credit based on what they know and are able to do. Students are directly assessed for competencies rather than using a proxy of learning such as seat time or credit hours. Reflecting the beliefs of many others in higher education, Tom Nielsen of Bellevue College stated, "We are introducing a disruptive model into the traditional college campus. Nothing will be the same once you take the time orientation off the table" (Poulin, 2015).

In a CBE program, learning experiences can be more personalized to students, as they are able to move at their own pace and blur traditional lines of education by integrating learning from multiple environments. In addition, learning is mostly assessed through performance assessments or direct assessments of what students know and are able to do. This complements the call for accountability to defined standards of quality based on what students know and can do, which helps explain why CBE is increasing in importance. The Competency-Based Education Network is a national consortium of campuses that are working together to develop scalable models of CBE. The lists of campuses involved along with the rapid increase of institutions joining the network are indications that CBE is on the rise. In fall 2015 the U.S. Department of Education is planning to launch competency-based experimental sites where 40 colleges will be able to administer programs without credit hour restrictions connected to student financial aid.

Student affairs must partner with academic affairs in the CBE movement. Such partnerships will greatly enhance the personalized student learning experience. One could argue that student affairs is actually better positioned to lead in a competency-based world. Every day, professionals facilitate applied learning experiences based on a defined set of competencies or outcomes. In student affairs, we don't have set courses or letter grades; professionals are directly assessing student learning in applied settings. This type of assessment will only increase as CBE spreads and creates a more seamless learning environment for students.

Comprehensive Transcripts

As assessment of student learning turns to more direct measures for students to demonstrate competency, advocates are calling for approaches that validate the learning that happens everywhere, arguing that all experiences while in pursuit of the degree should be included on the student record (most often the transcript). In addition, students and employers are looking for student records that better represent the range of learning that students accumulate. Institutions are experimenting with ways to document curricular and cocurricular learning to be able to provide a student record or transcript that is representative of the entirety of student competencies gained.

Student affairs professionals are already leading the charge to represent cocurricular learning on transcripts. For instance, Salt Lake Community College has students identify cocurricular experiences so faculty can assess the resultant learning and place the competencies on their transcripts. At Stanford, the Scholarship Record is an outcomes-based record of the cognitive skills students have learned, complementing the traditional academic transcript; at Elon University, the Elon Experiences Transcript documents students' experiences in experiential learning activities. Extending the transcript is another way for student affairs professionals to capitalize on this moment and further fulfill our mission and commitment to students by providing validation of the holistic learning students engage in both inside and outside the classroom.

Big Data Analytics

With the expanded use of technology, institutions are often data rich and analysis poor, meaning that data are often collected across the campus for long periods of time without any opportunity to make use of those data in analysis. If institutions are able to analyze patterns of student performance, persistence, and completion, major predictors of success could be determined. Data disaggregation allows these patterns to be broken down by student characteristics as broad as gender, race, or major, or as specific as on- or off-campus living, financial aid types, adviser influence, course attendance, campus activities involvement, or access to services such as counseling or the recreation center.

By mining data systems and integrating data from across the campus, many campuses are now warehousing large amounts of data to create data sets that provide comprehensive accounts of student behaviors and performance. As technology has emerged to pull all these data sources together and analytics have progressed to predictive models, strategic maps, and decision trees, campuses are now able to predict the student behaviors that most often lead to completion. As a result, early alert systems can allow instructors and advisers to follow up with students who are not engaging in those predictive behaviors. This provides real-time feedback and intervention for students to keep them on track to their goal of graduation before it is too late to intervene. It behooves student affairs professionals to be contributors to and consumers of big data analytics. Those divisions already invested in assessments are properly positioned to take advantage of and expand the use of big data.

Accountability Measures

The *U.S News & World Report* Best Colleges Ranking is one of the most publicly recognized lists of how universities and colleges may be measured for success. The data used to generate the rankings are based on such factors as presidents' and chief academic officers' perceptions of other colleges and universities and institutional characteristics such as financial resources, alumni giving, and selectivity. But as employers raise concerns about dismal graduation rates and the lack of preparation for the workforce among those who do graduate, there are new measures filling the marketplace.

In 2005, a new type of ranking emerged from the *Washington Monthly* that shifted the focus to three main areas of college and university work: (a) social mobility, based on the recruitment and graduation of low-income students; (b) research that examines scholarship and doctorates; and (c) service, meaning how the institution encourages students to give back. This ranking shows a shift in accountability that has been taking hold in the early twenty-first century. Student outcomes as a measure of ranking colleges have become a new way to consider college success.

Today it is clear that although these efforts are implemented with the best of intentions, they still do not meet the needs of students, families, employers, and legislators in holding colleges accountable for delivering on the social compact of a college degree for students. This shortcoming led President Barack Obama to propose a federal rating system, with access, affordability, and outcomes as measures. There has been speculation about tying the disbursement of federal student aid to the ratings and therefore increasing the role of the federal government in holding institutions accountable. Another measure that has advanced the conversation about using student outcomes is the Gallup-Purdue Index, which studies student outcomes after college and examines which practices contribute to graduates' success in finding good jobs and leading quality lives. The result of that study showed that long-term engagement and contentment at work was not determined by whether a college or university is public or private or even the expense involved in attending. What did matter were factors like caring professors, internships where students got to apply what they learned in class, and engagement in extracurricular activities and organizations. These kinds of results directly implicate the work of student affairs professionals and help us to understand why others will ask more questions about our work and demand more results. Those divisions of student affairs that develop, maintain, and sustain a culture of assessment will be much more likely to provide evidence-based answers to questions and challenges. Further, these approaches will enhance our ability to better accomplish that which we believe we already do.

Additionally, states are looking for ways to answer the cry for accountability by using performance- or outcomes-based funding. More than 30 state legislatures have passed policies that tie state appropriations for public institutions to student outcomes. These policies often connect a percentage of state funding for colleges to student indicators such as persistence, credits accrued, and completion. Every division within these colleges will be urged to contribute to the student success agenda in order to aid in gaining resources from the states. These state actions indicate that the pressure on student affairs to contribute to student retention, graduation, employment, and long-term contentment will only grow.

Looking Forward

There is widespread agreement that higher education is in the midst of a major transformation. Certainly, the very nature of the learning enterprise is changing. In the most recent Babson surveys of online learning, almost 50% of college undergraduates report taking at least one online class and 70% of chief academic officers say that online learning is critical for their institution's long-term strategy. Almost 75% of chief academic officers also think that outcomes for online learning are the same as or superior to traditional classroom learning (Babson Survey Research Group, 2014). At the same time the very nature of the credits, and even the freshman year, are being reconsidered and challenged. The emergence of CBE—the philosophy and structure in which students may receive credit for what they already know or can demonstrate through assessment measures—will challenge the very nature of the credit in a traditional classroom experience. Finally, innovations such as the Global Freshman Academy at Arizona State University change the traditional notions of the residentially based freshman-year experience. This program allows for an entirely online freshman course experience, at less than half the cost, before transferring into the traditional Arizona State University course program. Add to the mix the increase in dual-enrollment, advanced placement classes and other accelerated learning opportunities and you potentially alter the entire freshman-year experience. What changes when more and more students may enter our institutions as sophomores? How will that transform the traditional models we have of student affairs work and the process of documenting the contributions we make to higher education?

As these innovations begin to garner more widespread acceptance, it will be important for assessment professionals to understand the effect these new teaching and learning modalities have on key institutional outcomes. These data will need to be part of the dialogue about the efficacy of these new approaches and their overall impact on student success, degree progress, and completion. What is the impact on employability? Do these new innovations create success for all students across lines of race, gender, class, and socioeconomic status? Does a shortened academic experience affect learning outcomes for traditional, first-time, full-time college students? These and other related questions should be a key part of the new assessment agenda.

In addition to these "disruptive" trends in learning, the financial pressures in higher education over the past six years have resulted in an increasingly outcomes-based view of higher education by a range of stakeholders inside and outside of higher education. The majority of states now have some form of performance-based funding; that is, placing greater emphasis on funding that is tied to a set of metrics and outcomes. Another result of this fiscal pressure has been a consumer, "return-on-investment" view of higher education. Students, their parents, and potential employers all call for more attention to noncognitive or cross-cutting skills that are essential to a successful career. These skills, highly prized by employers and society in general, are often viewed as more important than students' majors or the colleges they attended. In fact, there is a growing disconnect between what colleges emphasize and what employers need, a development that does not serve either sector. Skills such as problem solving, teamwork, communication, critical thinking, creativity, leadership, collaboration, and intercultural skills are becoming *the* critical outcomes for the college experience. Unfortunately, measures of progress and mastery of these skills are often inadequate. The development of effective assessment strategies related to these skills will be increasingly important in the next decade.

Given the many challenges (or, perhaps with the right mind-set, opportunities) outlined here, it is not hard to see how student affairs (and higher education in general) needs to become more transformative. As outlined throughout this book there are some basic tenets of student affairs practice that must be held up as opportunities to position the field as relevant and contributory to the higher education enterprise. These tenets have implications for how assessment will be prioritized in student affairs looking toward the next decade:

1. Learning is a holistic experience. To this end, student affairs should be part of the overall campus assessment effort. It is essential that learning outside of the classroom in the rich mélange of students' lives be recognized as a vital part of the learning enterprise.

   > For this reason it is incumbent on student affairs to systematically assess the contributions to student learning outcomes of students' out-of-class experiences and of student affairs to these outcomes. Student affairs professionals should also be involved in the discussions that lead to the design and implementation of campuswide efforts to assess student learning and personal development and to use the results to improve the quality of the student experience. (Schuh & Gansemer-Topf, 2010, p. 6)

   It is important to note that although we must explore ways in which these out-of-class experiences facilitate and enrich classroom learning and success, it is equally important that student affairs assessment efforts not be entirely in the beyond-the-classroom arena.

2. To ensure credibility for student affairs assessment efforts, it will be important to develop more sophisticated direct measures of learning across the range of student affairs experiences. Although survey data will always play an important role in student affairs assessment, expanding our use of direct measures will add weight to the contributions the out-of-class experience plays in learning, degree progress, and completion. It's important to consider the accounts of how our students think that student affairs matters, but demonstrating how our stakeholders can enact strategies for managing college and life differently as a result of our work is also vital.

3. Given the budget and fiscal constraints that have and will continue to affect higher education in the coming years, it is critical that student affairs leaders adopt an assessment-centered approach to program development and evaluation. Programs, staffing decisions, and resource allocation should be data driven and based on comprehensive assessment efforts. Every program or resource should link directly to core strategic goals and learning outcomes.

4. Big data and data analytics have come to higher education in a major way in the past few years. For example, on the academic side, data from learning management systems are being used in early and proactive advising systems that are having a positive effect on student persistence. Equally, there is a wealth of data in the student affairs world including "one-card" usage, student activity engagment, and participation in recreation and community activities that will be valuable in understanding patterns of

behavior that relate to student success. Student affairs could benefit from an increased emphasis on data analytics that would address two key questions: "Where are we losing our students?" and "What experiences are connected to student success?"

5. Student affairs professionals should fully examine the potential for extended transcripts, cocurricular transcripts, badging, and electronic portfolios as emerging ways to document learning. Market forces from companies such as LinkedIn necessitate that colleges develop robust, technology-based systems that allow students to reflect, plan, and document their learning. This is even more important given the discussion of noncognitive learning outcomes discussed earlier.

These and other challenges will need to be a major focus for student affairs leadership. Assessment is at the very heart of the future of student affairs. Therefore, assessment in student affairs work becomes a core professional competency and critical strategic planning tool; it should be the foundation upon which all of the programs and services within student affairs are based.

Call to Action

The time is now for all student affairs practitioners to engage in discussion about these topics and begin to think differently about their work. Stan Carpenter, in his foreword to *Learning Is Not a Sprint* (Collins & Roberts, 2012), stated that professionals "have to be able to articulate the reasons for our existence and our contributions to the educational enterprise. . . . It is past time to get serious about this" (p. ix). As demonstrated previously, policy and practice changes to drive reforms are already in place and will only continue to grow; they are not futuristic in the sense that these are projections about changes to come in 10 to 15 years. The time to take action is now.

As an SSAO, consider the ways that you can begin to use the ten tenets or expand on them in order to lead on these issues. The practical guidance provided in this book is focused on creating a student-centered, learning-based experience that will help leaders not only be successful in navigating change but also thrive in that effort. From grounding your leadership in the purpose and meaning of student affairs and committing to student learning (Chapters 1 and 2) to creating and sustaining an assessment culture (Chapters 3–6) that engages staff in using evidence to design practices that lead to increased student success, the advice provided from peers gives you insight into how you can take the first steps, revisit current efforts, or start new initiatives that will prepare your division for the work ahead. Then, once the work is under way, you have expert advice in Chapters 7 through 10 about specific practices in assessment whose soundness has been demonstrated, so you can plan for assessment, recognize quality evidence, and communicate effectively about the work of the division. These actions will greatly enhance your division's ability to overcome the challenges and reap the rewards of assessment.

References

Babson Survey Research Group. (2014). *Grade level: tracking online education in the United States*. Retrieved from http://onlinelearningconsortium.org/read/survey-reports-2014/

Collins, K., & Roberts, D. (2012). *Learning is not a sprint: Assessing and documenting student leader learning in co-curricular involvement*. Washington, DC: National Association of Student Personnel Administrators.

Poulin, R. (2015). *Implementing a CBE program: Lessons learned from community colleges*. Retrieved from https://wcetblog.wordpress.com/2015/06/11/implementing-a-cbe-program-lessons-learned-from-community-colleges/

Schuh, J. H., and Gansemer-Topf, A. M. (2010). *The role of student affairs in student learning assessment* (NILOA Occasional Paper). Champaign, IL: National Institute for Learning Outcomes Assessment.

ABOUT THE CONTRIBUTORS

Javaune Adams-Gaston is vice president for student life at The Ohio State University, where she has broad leadership responsibility for more than 40 operations affecting more than 62,000 students' learning and development outside of the classroom. She provides comprehensive university leadership and is a member of the university's senior administration. In more than 20 years of experience in higher education and student affairs, she has been a member of graduate faculty (University of Maryland, Johns Hopkins University, and The Ohio State University) and has enjoyed leadership roles in a broad variety of areas including counseling, career services, diversity and inclusion, athletics, academic affairs, and student affairs. Adams-Gaston currently serves on the board of trustees at the University of Dubuque, the board of directors at St. Stephens Community House, and the board of directors for the American Red Cross, Central Ohio Region. She is the recipient of numerous awards, including the Diamond Honoree Award, the highest honor of the American College Personnel Association. Adams-Gaston has a PhD in psychology from Iowa State University.

James P. Barber is assistant professor of education at the College of William & Mary in Williamsburg, Virginia. Prior to joining the faculty, he served as a student affairs administrator, working in the areas of fraternity and sorority affairs, residence life, and student activities. Barber's teaching and research focus on student learning and development, with a particular interest in the integration of learning—the ways in which students make connections among ideas, skills, and knowledge across contexts. His research has appeared in the *American Educational Research Journal*, the *Journal of College Student Development*, and the *Journal of Higher Education*. He earned his PhD from the Center for the Study of Higher and Postsecondary Education at the University of Michigan.

Rosie Phillips Bingham is vice president for student affairs and a tenured professor at the University of Memphis. Bingham has served on several editorial boards, including the board for the *Journal of College Student Development* and currently serves on the board for the *Journal of Career Assessment*. She has served as president of the Association of University and College

151

Counseling Center Directors, the International Association of Counseling Services, and the Society of Counseling Psychology of the American Psychological Association. In her senior student affairs officer role she has sought to create a culture of evidence grounded in student learning. She has challenged all staff to add learning objectives and assessment to each year's plans for programs and services. As a result, programs have grown and positively impacted retention and graduation. In 2015, Bingham was named a "Pillar of the Profession" by the NASPA Foundation Board. She earned her doctorate in counseling psychology from The Ohio State University.

Stephanie Blaisdell is the assistant vice president of student affairs at the University of Memphis. Blaisdell oversees student development, which includes student affairs learning and assessment, campus recreation and intramural services, career services, commencement, disability resources for students, educational support programs, the First Scholars Program for first-generation students, student health and counseling, and student success programs (two student support services grants). Blaisdell represents the division of student affairs in university strategic planning and accreditation and coleads the university's degree completion committee. She previously served as the director of student affairs learning and assessment at the University of Memphis and prior to that was the director of diversity and women's programs at Worcester Polytechnic Institute and director of women in science and engineering programs at Arizona State University. Blaisdell's research focuses on career and academic self-efficacy for women in STEM fields, and she is the author of over 20 peer reviewed articles on the topic. She holds a PhD in counseling psychology from Arizona State University.

Daniel A. Bureau is the director of student affairs learning and assessment and the special assistant to the vice president for student affairs at the University of Memphis. In his 20 years of work in student affairs, he has worked in a range of functional areas including student leadership and fraternity and sorority life programs and has consulted on more than 30 campuses. He has served professional associations in numerous roles including as part of the board of directors for the Council for the Advancement of Standards (CAS). He has a PhD in higher education and student affairs from Indiana University.

Emily Burris Hester serves as the assistant to the vice president for the department of Student Life & Enrollment at Louisiana State University where she coordinates division-wide assessment and retention efforts. Previously, Burris Hester worked for Delta Gamma Fraternity and worked on the

ResponseAbility Project educating college students about bystander behavior. She received an MA in higher education/student affairs from Louisiana State University.

Todd Chamberlain is the director of planning and assessment for the division of student affairs at Clemson University. Prior to his work at Clemson, he was assistant director of the Center for Postsecondary Research at Indiana University Bloomington, where he managed administration of the National Survey of Student Engagement and its affiliated surveys. In addition to his student affairs experience in residence life, orientation, and student activities, he has been involved in NASPA and served on ACPA's Commission for Admissions, Orientation, and the First-Year Experience. He has a PhD in higher education and student affairs from Indiana University.

Michael N. Christakis serves as vice president for student affairs and a public service professor at the State University of New York at Albany. Since his arrival at the university in 1999, Christakis has served in numerous positions in student affairs, most recently serving as associate vice president for student affairs. As a member of the vice president's staff since 2007, Christakis developed assessment and evaluation practices; improved the effectiveness of divisional planning, professional development, communications, and risk management; and provided oversight to critical campus life areas including student involvement and leadership, the Campus Center, and campus recreation. In July 2012, he was elected national president for Omicron Delta Kappa and also serves as the president for university auxiliary services at the University at Albany. In March 2015, Christakis was elected national co-chair of NASPA's Assessment, Evaluation, and Research Knowledge Community. Christakis holds a PhD from the Rockefeller College of Public Affairs and Policy at the University at Albany.

Marylee Demeter is director of assessment for Cumberland County College, where she is responsible for providing leadership and professional development to support college-wide assessment activities in the areas of academics, administration, and student affairs. Prior to assuming her current role, Demeter served as coordinator of student affairs assessment and research at Rutgers University, as well as part-time lecturer for the Graduate School of Education, where she developed and facilitated an online course in applied student affairs assessment for graduate students in the college student affairs program. Demeter previously served as adjunct faculty member for the history and social sciences department at Middlesex County College, where she taught courses in educational psychology, student success development, and lifespan development. In addition, she provides consultation in research and statistics in the areas of education and nursing research. She earned an EdM in educational measurement, statistics, and program evaluation and an MA in educational psychology from the Graduate School of Education at Rutgers University.

Amber Garrison Duncan serves as evaluation officer and strategy officer at the Lumina Foundation. Her work focuses on managing evaluations and applying findings to inform Lumina's work to reach Goal 2025. She also serves on Lumina's strategy work group on new systems of quality credentials in higher education, including the Degree Qualifications Profile and Tuning. These activities allow her to draw on her 15 years of experience as a campus-based student affairs professional, designing cocurricular learning experiences and leading assessment. Garrison Duncan has served in leadership roles with NASPA, ACPA, and Student Affairs Assessment Leaders. She earned a PhD in educational leadership at the University of Oregon and has researched and written on student affairs assessment, general education, women in higher education, and Latina student experiences in college.

Robin H. Holmes is vice president for student life at the University of Oregon. Her division leads the university's efforts in prevention, student learning, social engagement, career development, leadership, and service learning. Holmes has worked at the University of Oregon since 1992. She served as dean of students and director of the University Counseling and Testing Center prior to her appointment as vice president. She has taught classes and workshops on multiculturalism, multicultural competencies in therapy, and cross-cultural dynamics in conflict medication, as well as identity formation and development. In 2007, Holmes was named one of 39 American Council on Education Fellows in which capacity she served as an administrative fellow at the University of California, Berkeley in the office of the chancellor and the vice chancellor for equity and diversity. Holmes holds a PhD from the California School of Professional Psychology and is a licensed clinical psychologist.

Lance C. Kennedy-Phillips is vice provost for planning and assessment at Pennsylvania State University. Prior to joining Pennsylvania State University, Lance served as associate vice provost for institutional research at the University of Illinois at Chicago. He is also the founding executive director of the Center for the Study of Student Life at The Ohio State University. Kennedy-Phillips has held faculty positions at The Ohio State University, Clemson University, and DePaul University teaching graduate level courses in research methods, strategic planning, and assessment practices in higher education.

Kennedy-Phillips is a nationally recognized speaker on topics related to outcomes assessment, higher education policy, strategic planning, and organizational learning. In 2010 he served as coeditor of the book *Qualitative & Quantitative Research: A Mixed Methods Approach in Higher Education (Prentice Hall, 2010).* Kennedy-Phillips has authored or coauthored nearly 20 book chapters and peer reviewed publications. He is an active member of both the Association for Institutional Research (AIR) and NASPA-Student Affairs Administrators in Higher Education. Recently, he served as national co-chair for the NASPA Assessment, Research, and Evaluation Knowledge Community from 2010 to 2013 and director of the Foundations I Institute for the Association for Institutional Research from 2008 to 2012. Kennedy-Phillips earned his PhD from the University of Nebraska.

Kurt J. Keppler serves as vice president for the department of Student Life & Enrollment at Louisiana State University. Previously, Keppler served as vice president for student affairs at Valdosta State University, associate vice president and dean of students at Georgia State University, associate dean of student affairs at Virginia Commonwealth University, and assistant director of student development at the University of Missouri. He held adjunct teaching positions at each institution and has taught leadership seminars and courses in group dynamics, organizational behavior, and leadership theory. He was the 2005–2006 president of the National Association of Student Personnel Administrators and was named a NASPA "Pillar of the Profession" in 2007. Keppler has made more than 150 presentations at state, regional, and national conferences and has consulted on more than 30 college campuses. He coedited NASPA's 2005 monograph, *Partnering with the Parents of Today's College Students.* Keppler has a PhD from the University of Missouri.

Kevin Kruger is the first executive-level president of NASPA, representing NASPA in national forums such as the Washington Higher Education Secretariat. In his capacity as a national advocate for students and the primary spokesperson for student affairs administrators and practitioners, he draws on more than 30 years of experience in higher education. He worked for 15 years at the University of Maryland College Park and the University of Maryland Baltimore County. During his tenure at the University of Maryland, Kruger worked in orientation, student activities, leadership development, admissions, and with the vice president for student affairs office. Kruger has also served as an adjunct faculty member in the Student Development in Higher Education program at Trinity College in Washington, DC.

Marilee J. Bresciani Ludvik serves as professor of postsecondary educational leadership at San Diego State University, where she coordinates the master's in postsecondary educational leadership in student affairs, the minor for multidisciplinary leadership, the mindfulness-based integrative inquiry program, and the certificate for institutional research, planning, and assessment. Ludvik's most recent research focuses on using translational neuroscience to inform the design and evaluation of workshops and curriculum to decrease student, faculty, and administrator stress and anxiety and increase each group's attention, emotion, and cognitive regulation, as well as enhance their critical thinking, compassion, and creativity. Ludvik has a PhD in administration, curriculum, and instruction with emphasis in higher education from the University of Nebraska.

Darby Roberts is the director of student life studies in the division of student affairs at Texas A&M University. Before assuming her role in student affairs assessment, she worked in residence life and student organization advising. Roberts was a founding member of Student Affairs Assessment Leaders and was co-chair of the NASPA Assessment, Evaluation, and Research Knowledge Community. She is a frequent presenter and consultant at institutions across the country and teaches in the student affairs administration and higher education master's program at Texas A&M University. Roberts has written about student affairs assessment issues, including as coauthor of the 2012 book *Learning Is Not a Sprint: Assessing and Documenting Student Leader Learning in Cocurricular Involvement.* She earned her PhD in higher education administration from Texas A&M University.

William D. Schafer has served as the vice president for student life at West Virginia University since January 2015. From 2004 to 2015, he served as the vice president for student affairs at Georgia Institute of Technology. Schafer has also served in roles as associate vice president and dean of students at University of Texas at El Paso, dean of student life at the University of Denver, and dean of students at the Illinois Institute of Technology. He also served as director of the office of student conduct and other student offices at the University of Colorado Boulder. During his 35-year career, he has been responsible for more than 30 different student services departments. He has also been part of several national organizations including the Association of Public and Land-Grant Universities (APLU), serving as a cochief student affairs officer, and the National Association of Student Personnel Administrators (NASPA). Schafer earned a PhD in higher education administration and curriculum from the University of Colorado Boulder.

Vicki L. Wise is currently the associate director for teaching, learning, and assessment in the office of academic innovation at Portland State University. Vicki has also served as director for assessment and research in student affairs at Portland State University. Prior to joining Portland State University, she worked at James Madison University as director of assessment and evaluation for the College of Education, assistant director for institutional research, and assistant professor/research administrator in the Center for Assessment and Research Studies. In her 25 years in higher education assessment, her passion has been to assist faculty and staff to design and assess programs and services that facilitate student learning and development. She has served in numerous volunteer/consultancy roles, including as chair and co-chair of ACPA's Assessment Institute, chair and co-chair of Student Affairs Assessment Leaders (SAAL), and on the editorial board for *Research & Practice in Assessment*. She is one of the cofounders of the Oregon Assessment Conference in Student Affairs. She earned her PhD in psychological and cultural studies from the University of Nebraska.

Brenda "B" Woods is the director of research and assessment for student affairs with faculty status at the Georgia Institute of Technology. In her 27 years of work in student affairs she has held leadership positions in assessment, research and evaluation, housing, student conduct, new student orientation, and the student center. Woods has made more than 80 presentations at state, regional, and national conferences and has consulted on more than 20 college campuses. Her areas of expertise include student affairs assessment, alcohol and other drug abuse prevention and education, crime and campus security, destructive cults, and sexual assault theory and prevention. She has served as the associate dean of students at Texas Tech University with a teaching position in the College of Education and as a research evaluator at Harvard University. Woods earned her PhD in higher education administration from Texas Tech University.